JOURNEY BY EXCURSION TRAIN FRO

EAST

LANCASHI

----- PART ONE -----

COLNE, NELSON, BURNLEY, ACCRINGTON & BLACKBURN

Wackersall Bridge 15th June 1963. B1 4-6-0 No.**61024** *Addax*, (a rare choice of engine for an excursion from Colne) rattles over the pointwork at Wackersall Bridge as it leaves Colne with 1T52, the 11.40am Colne to Blackpool. This loco. had arrived at Colne the previous night with the 9.15pm passenger from Blackpool, a train noted for its wide range of motive power. *Brian Wrigglesworth.*

STUART TAYLOR

ISBN 1 870119 35 5

Edited by Gregory K. Fox
Typeset by Bill Rear, Johnstown, Wrexham
Printed by the Amadeus Press, Huddersfield

Published by Foxline Publishing
32, Urwick Road, Romiley, Stockport. SK6 3JS

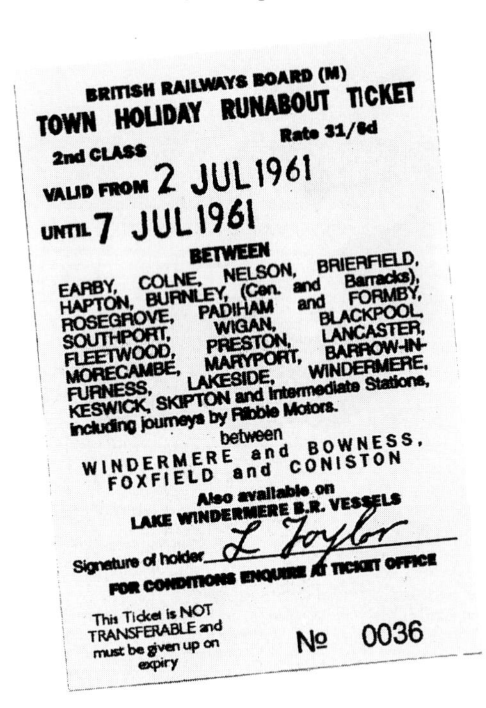
BRITISH RAILWAYS BOARD (M)
TOWN HOLIDAY RUNABOUT TICKET
2nd CLASS Rate 31/6d
VALID FROM 2 JUL 1961
UNTIL 7 JUL 1961
BETWEEN
EARBY, COLNE, NELSON, BRIERFIELD, HAPTON, BURNLEY, (Cen. and Barracks), ROSEGROVE, PADIHAM and FORMBY, SOUTHPORT, WIGAN, BLACKPOOL, FLEETWOOD, PRESTON, LANCASTER, MORECAMBE, MARYPORT, BARROW-IN-FURNESS, LAKESIDE, WINDERMERE, KESWICK, SKIPTON and intermediate Stations, including journeys by Ribble Motors.
between
WINDERMERE and BOWNESS, FOXFIELD and CONISTON
Also available on
LAKE WINDERMERE B.R. VESSELS
Signature of holder L Taylor
FOR CONDITIONS ENQUIRE AT TICKET OFFICE
This Ticket is NOT TRANSFERABLE and must be given up on expiry
№ 0036

Contents ...

4216 2nd-SINGLE SINGLE-2nd 4216
Blackburn to
Blackburn Blackpool
BLACKPOOL
(M) 7/9 Fare 7/9 (M)
For conditions see over

DAY EXCURSION -2nd 0692
Southport (Chapel Street) to HOGHTON
Fare 4/6 (M)
For conditions see over

Bonnie Colne

Southport excursion. Rose Grove's Black five No.**45196** rests at Colne in the warm summer sun on Saturday 5th June 1965 awaiting departure with the 12 noon excursion to Southport.The young lad in the cab looks very much like Rose Grove fireman Derek Moody. *A.C.Gilbert.*

Acknowledgements.

Sincere thanks are given to the following people without whom, this book would simply not have been possible.

Railwaymen. Peter Baughan, Colin Boocock, John Deluca, Neil Godwin, Ron Graham, Norman Harling, Ron Herbert, Terry Kershaw, Luke Kaye, Mick Kelly, Eric Laycock, Mark Marshall, Des. Melia, Ron Parkinson, Vinny Staffa, Ray Thorpe, Allan Tillotson, Frank Watson, the late Len Wesson.
Photographers etc. Duncan Armstrong, Barry Atkinson, Gordon Biddle, Eddie Bobrowski, Bernard Bond, David Carter, Noel Coates, Dave Dyson, Michael Feather, Peter Fitton, A.C. Gilbert, R.S. Greenwood, Jimmy Heap, Bert Holland, Bill Hurst, Stuart James, Peter A. Lord, Leo Moore, Brian Morrison, G.H.Platt, John E. Porter, Tim Proctor and the archives of The Colne Times newspaper, Geoff Robinson, Raymond Short, Don Speak, Bob Spencer, Mr & Mrs Standaloft, Ken Stout, Brian Wrigglesworth, The E.Blakey and J.Robinson collections courtesy of The L & Y Society, via Noel Coates. Stanley Duxburys pictures by kind permission of Mrs. Sandra England. The assistance given by Lancashire Libraries is greatly appreciated and special thanks are given to Christine Bradley and the staff at Colne also to Mrs. Barrett at the Accrington reference dept., John Bettle of Railtrack ILM for assistance with plans.

Enginemen elite. Two of the best !, fireman Terry Kershaw and driver John Deluca. *Terry Kershaw.*

Introduction.

Holiday excursion trains from East Lancashire in the 1950s, who at the time would have thought that some 40 years on there would be a serious interest in the events surrounding those hectic summer days out in the 1950s. Those memorable trips by rail to seaside stations, now long gone, travelling over routes that have been closed some 30 years and using locomotives and coaching stock, which are now ,just a fading memory. The impressions made upon this young lad from Colne by those holiday train journeys must surely have helped to mould my ideas ambitions and outlook over the years. My association with the railways has lasted many years both in interest and employment, but I do not consider myself an enthusiast and I have little time for today's railway, which is merely a shadow of what existed in the 1950s. As a youngster in the 50s, I marvelled at the apparent teamwork of the various staff, how they took all the busy holiday trains in their stride, coping with many thousands of extra passengers throughout the summer season from May until September.

Year after year the excursion trains ran like clockwork, using similar timings and often the same train codes, in many cases even the same staff would be seen working the specials, though there was always a steady turnover in young lads as firemen on the steamers. (shifts and girlfriends don't go together!). I started on the railway not with the usual intention of becoming a train driver, it was purely to see what all the teamwork was about, to grasp an inside view of the old style of railway working before it was completely eroded away by modern practices. Thankfully, I was lucky enough to do this and it was surprising just how much atmosphere lingered over the years despite the changes that would come in the 1960s.

Many years ago when we had quite a lot of spare turns at the depot, I began seriously writing notes about those happy holiday journeys in the 1950s, not for any particular reason, merely that I felt as time progressed my own recollections of those days would begin to fade. My fears were however unfounded and I am luckily blessed with a very keen memory for events, in fact "truly vivid" at times. The Taylor family outings to the Lancashire seaside resorts in the 1950s and early 60s, would involve dad, (Leslie), mum (Doris) and brother Herbert better known as Bert, whilst I was known to all and sundry as "Our Copper", a name I received as a result of the many shades of red and brown that my hair was coloured in those days, all of which I might add, were natural. Most of the excursion journeys by train to Blackpool and Southport etc. would be in the region of 1 hour 50 minutes to just over 2 hours in duration, stops being made at 6 or 7 stations along the route through East Lancashire to pick up further passengers. All the journeys to the seaside were fascinating as we rarely in those days ventured anywhere other than at the local holiday periods, so each trip was an adventure to us. Taking engine numbers along the way probably began with dad assuming that we would be bored on these daily outings. Far from it, there was too much to see for it to be anything like that. Dad would usually be the "number-taker" whilst Bert and myself manned each side of the compartment and we would shout out the locomotives numbers as we journeyed along, thankfully a number of the little notepads we used have survived. They display the facts that a wide range of motive power could be seen in action in East and West Lancashire at that time. There is no way that we can compare the lifestyles and ideals of today with the way we were in the 1950s. We worked hard and played hard and by that I mean we were generally more active, energetic and out going. We did things in a community atmosphere, queuing was a British way of life, be it for a train the cinema or shops etc. Holidays were no exception and they were far more a social event in the 1950s than they are today. Now we are all looking for secluded beaches on some foreign island. Back in the 50s we would simply take our chances amongst the many thousands who lined the sands on the Golden Mile at Blackpool. The words of George Formby's song "Blackpool Prom" are laughable but there was a great deal of truth in them, certainly in the 1950s. This is the way George put it " ... I'VE JUST BEEN ON MY HOLIDAYS TO BLACKPOOL BY THE SEA AND ALTHOUGH I'M FEELING MIGHTY FIT, MY FEET ARE TROUBLING ME...., I QUEUED FOR HOURS AND HOURS, BUT I MUST SAY IT WAS GRAND, TO GET AS NEAR AS HALF A MILE, TO SEVERAL MILES OF SAND.....!

With the aid of my notes and memories together with some really smashing photographs of the railway routes through East Lancashire in the 1950s and 60s, we are going to re-live those excursion trips once more. We will travel from Colne to Burnley and on to Rose Grove, passing the busy marshalling yards there. We will also be taking a trip over the long closed route via Padiham to Great Harwood, after which we shall journey round via Accrington and Rishton to reach Blackburn, our ultimate destination in this volume being Bamber Bridge. There will be the occasional look at the railway staff in East Lancashire and on the way we'll learn a few things about some of the workers that will cause a chuckle or two. This look at the holiday trains from East Lancashire is designed to be a relaxing but informative guide, rather than a stuffy history book that constantly refers to the construction closure and demolition dates of the railway system in the area. For me the only tinge of sadness is that so many of the people who travelled on those excursion train are no longer with us, including my own parents. They would dearly have loved to look back at those happy times, when life was so simple. I know for a fact that mum would have been in her element over a book of this nature. Whilst en-route to the seaside she would often break into song reciting a chorus of George Formby's "With My Little Stick Of Blackpool Rock" at this point dad would usually stare out of the compartment window trying to give the impression that he really wasn't travelling with this loony crowd ...!

Finally I feel it is only fitting to fully acknowledge the assistance given to me by both railway staff and photographers etc.,all of whom were ever willing to help in any way possible. Finding the many pictures to illustrate excursion trains in East Lancashire proved a daunting task and some of the requests made to these most helpful people really took some believing to say the least. The enthusiasm shown by the contributors matched my own endeavours and as a result it ensured that the widest range of pictures were available for use and that the details and information is both plentiful and accurate ...... THANK YOU ONE AND ALL .

Stuart Taylor
Colne
April 1995.

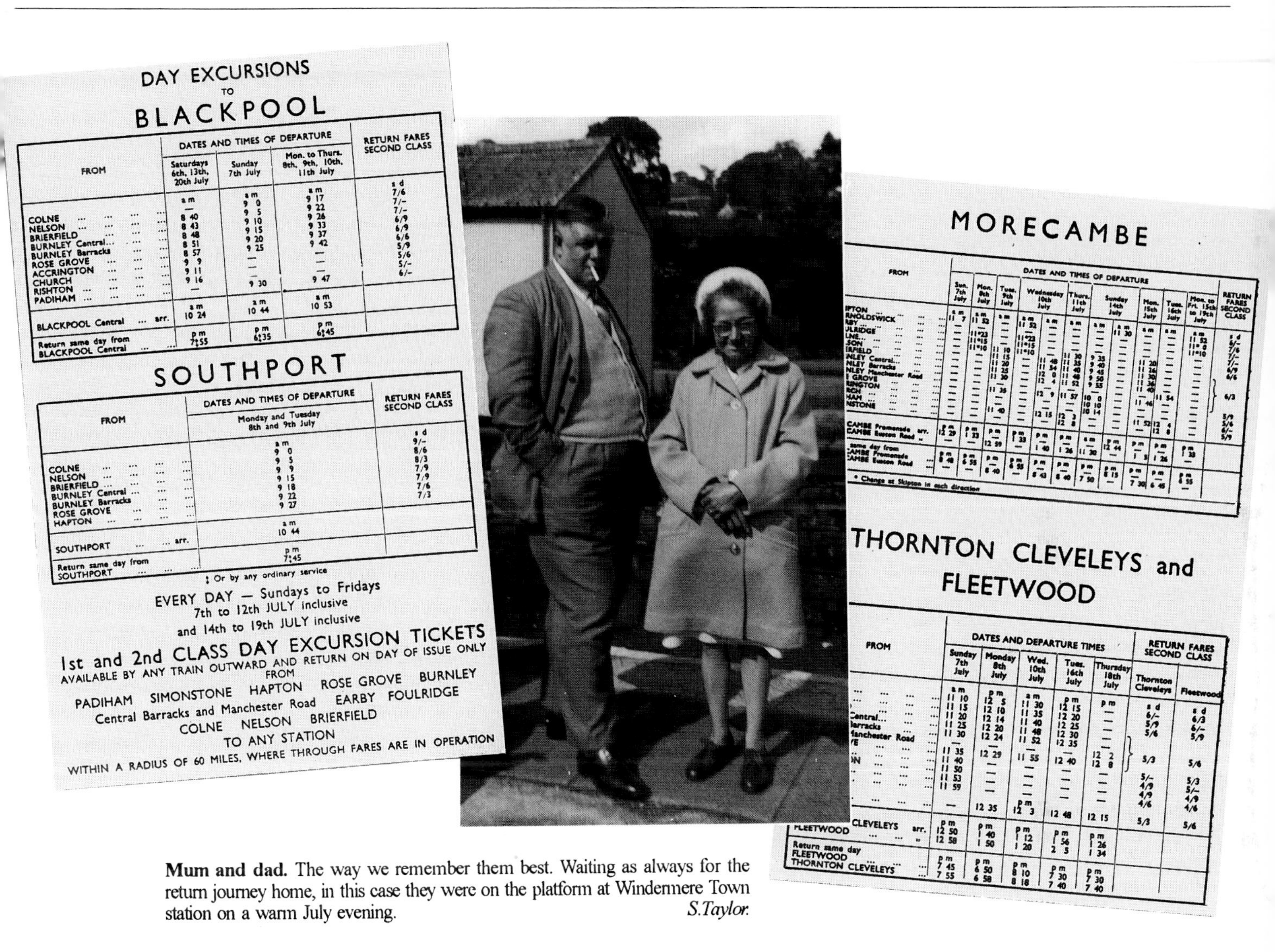

DAY EXCURSIONS
TO
BLACKPOOL

FROM	DATES AND TIMES OF DEPARTURE			RETURN FARES SECOND CLASS
	Saturdays 6th, 13th, 20th July	Sunday 7th July	Mon. to Thurs. 8th, 9th, 10th, 11th July	
	a m	a m	a m	s d
COLNE	—	9 0	9 17	7/6
NELSON	8 40	9 5	9 22	7/-
BRIERFIELD	8 43	9 10	9 26	7/-
BURNLEY Central	8 48	9 15	9 33	6/9
BURNLEY Barracks	8 51	9 20	9 37	6/9
ROSE GROVE	8 57	9 25	9 42	6/6
ACCRINGTON	9 9	—	—	5/9
CHURCH	9 11	—	—	5/6
RISHTON	9 16	—	—	5/-
PADIHAM	—	9 30	9 47	6/-
BLACKPOOL Central ... arr.	a m 10 24	a m 10 44	a m 10 53	
Return same day from BLACKPOOL Central	p m 7‡55	p m 6‡35	p m 6‡45	

SOUTHPORT

FROM	DATES AND TIMES OF DEPARTURE	RETURN FARES SECOND CLASS
	Monday and Tuesday 8th and 9th July	
	a m	s d
COLNE	9 0	9/-
NELSON	9 5	8/6
BRIERFIELD	9 9	8/3
BURNLEY Central	9 15	7/9
BURNLEY Barracks	9 18	7/9
ROSE GROVE	9 22	7/6
HAPTON	9 27	7/3
SOUTHPORT ... arr.	a m 10 44	
Return same day from SOUTHPORT	p m 7‡45	

‡ Or by any ordinary service

EVERY DAY — Sundays to Fridays
7th to 12th JULY inclusive
and 14th to 19th JULY inclusive

1st and 2nd CLASS DAY EXCURSION TICKETS
AVAILABLE BY ANY TRAIN OUTWARD AND RETURN ON DAY OF ISSUE ONLY
FROM
PADIHAM SIMONSTONE HAPTON ROSE GROVE BURNLEY
Central Barracks and Manchester Road EARBY FOULRIDGE
COLNE NELSON BRIERFIELD
TO ANY STATION
WITHIN A RADIUS OF 60 MILES, WHERE THROUGH FARES ARE IN OPERATION

MORECAMBE

FROM	Sun. 7th July	Mon. 8th July	Tues. 9th July	Wednesday 10th July	Wednesday 10th July	Thurs. 11th July	Sunday 14th July	Sunday 14th July	Mon. 15th July	Tues. 16th July	Mon. to Fri. 15th to 19th July	RETURN FARES SECOND CLASS
	a m	a m	a m	a m	a m	a m	a m	a m	a m	a m	a m	s d
IPTON	11 7	11 52	—	11 52	—	—	—	11 30	—	—	11 52	6/-
RNOLDSWICK	—	—	—	—	—	—	—	—	—	—	11*0	7/6
RBY	—	11*23	—	11*23	—	—	—	—	—	—	11*10	7/-
ULRIDGE	—	11*15	—	11*15	—	—	—	—	—	—	—	7/-
LNE	—	11*10	11 10	11*10	—	11 30	9 35	—	11 20	—	—	6/9
SON	—	—	11 15	—	11 48	11 35	9 40	—	11 26	—	—	6/6
ERFIELD	—	—	11 20	—	11 54	11 40	9 45	—	11 30	—	—	6/3
NLEY Central	—	—	11 25	—	12 0	11 48	9 50	—	11 36	—	—	6/3
NLEY Barracks	—	—	11 30	—	12 4	11 52	9 55	—	11 40	—	—	6/3
NLEY Manchester Road	—	—	—	—	—	—	—	—	—	11 54	—	6/3
E GROVE	—	—	11 35	—	12 9	11 57	10 0	—	11 46	—	—	6/3
RINGTON	—	—	—	—	—	—	10 10	—	—	—	—	5/9
RCH	—	—	—	—	—	—	10 14	—	—	—	—	5/6
HAM	—	—	11 40	—	12 15	12 3	—	—	11 52	12 4	—	6/-
NSTONE	—	—	—	—	—	12 8	—	—	—	12 8	—	5/9
CAMBE Promenade arr.	p m 12 29	p m 1 33	p m —	p m 1 33	p m —	p m —	a m —	p m 12 44	p m —	p m —	p m 1 33	
CAMBE Euston Road "	—	—	12 59	—	1 40	1 26	11 30	—	1 5	1 26	—	
same day from CAMBE Promenade	p m 8 48	p m 6 55	p m —	p m 6 55	p m —	p m —	p m —	p m 8 15	p m —	p m —	p m 6 55	
CAMBE Euston Road	—	—	8 40	—	8 43	8 40	7 50	—	7 30	6 45	—	

* Change at Skipton in each direction

THORNTON CLEVELEYS and FLEETWOOD

FROM	Sunday 7th July	Monday 8th July	Wed. 10th July	Tues. 16th July	Thursday 18th July	Thornton Cleveleys	Fleetwood
	a m	p m	a m	p m	p m	s d	s d
	11 10	12 5	11 30	12 15	—	6/-	6/3
	11 15	12 10	11 35	12 20	—	5/9	6/-
	11 20	12 14	11 40	12 25	—	5/6	5/9
Central...	11 25	12 20	11 48	12 30	—	5/3	5/6
Barracks	11 30	12 24	11 52	12 35	—	5/3	5/6
Manchester Road	—	—	—	—	12 2	5/3	5/6
VE	11 35	12 29	11 55	12 40	12 8	5/3	5/6
	11 40	—	—	—	—	5/-	5/3
ON	11 50	—	—	—	—	4/9	5/-
	11 53	—	—	—	—	4/9	4/9
	11 59	—	—	—	—	4/6	4/6
	—	12 35	p m 12 3	12 48	12 15	5/3	5/6
CLEVELEYS arr.	p m 12 50	p m 1 40	p m 1 12	p m 1 56	p m 1 26		
FLEETWOOD "	12 58	1 50	1 20	2 5	1 34		
Return same day FLEETWOOD	p m 7 45	p m 6 50	p m 8 10	p m 7 30	p m 7 30		
THORNTON CLEVELEYS	7 55	6 58	8 18	7 40	7 40		

Mum and dad. The way we remember them best. Waiting as always for the return journey home, in this case they were on the platform at Windermere Town station on a warm July evening. *S.Taylor.*

Dedication

To mum and dad,

I would like to dedicate the two parts of these excursion volumes to my parents Leslie and Doris Taylor. Thanks to their energetic approach to day tripping, brother Bert and myself were treated to many enjoyable rail journeys all those years ago. Dad, always the father figure, would plan the outings with military precision, organising the "roster" of which trains we would catch and when etc. He was totally in control, ever confident in all situations. To dad all railway staff were called "Jock", a nickname, surprisingly, to which they all readily answered, be they guards drivers porters etc. and my abiding memory of dad is as we sat on the excursion platforms at Blackpool Central, already tucked in our non-corridor compartment up near the front of the train. He would give a shrill whistle to gain the attention of the man pushing the tea trolley back and forth along the platform. Hearing the whistle the young man would look up, it was then that dad would bellow the familiar line "Over here Jock" and up would dash the white coated figure, his tea trolley loaded with goodies, "What's it to be Guv" the man would ask. It was just like a scene from a 1940s film where the troops are setting off for war. It is not surprising therefore that on many of these return journeys from the seaside that dad would often drift off into lengthy tales about his wartime exploits and the troubles of trying to get back home whilst on leave. Mum, like dad, was forever easy going and "going" was the operative word as far as mum was concerned. Mum always delighted in those outings by rail and if you gave her a comfy non-corridor compartment, a flask of coffee and some sandwiches then her face would be a picture of serenity mile after mile as we headed for the seaside. Life in postwar Britain was drab to say the least, more so in Lancashire mill towns such as Colne. It was no wonder therefore that when the holidays came along people tended to let their hair down and mum and dad were no exception. They toiled long and hard to ensure that we all had a holiday to remember and it clearly must have worked! Some 35 - 40 years later the memories of those day trips by train to the Lancashire Coast are as vivid as ever.

Setting the scene.

For many of us, the post war years of the 1950s will remain etched in our memories, especially the holiday periods. A general atmosphere of austerity still prevailed for much of the 50s and although we didn't realise it at the time, big changes were definitely on the way.
In the few short years from 1955 to 1965, our ideas, living standards, expectations, particularly our holiday choices would change quite dramatically even here in the mill towns of Lancashire. When it came to holiday transport in the 1950s, a small percentage of people would use the growing motor coach services offered by the coach firms of Ribble and Standerwick, as well as Helen Smiths of Rochdale and Robinson Bros. of Blackburn. Incidentally, the local coach firm in Colne was Bracewell and Mittons. An even smaller percentage of holidaymakers would be lucky enough to operate their own vehicles at this period in time, but by far the largest percentage of the travelling public in those post war years would be catered for by the railways. The mid 1950s marked the approach of the busiest "excursion years" that the railways of East Lancashire would ever see. In a period of less than ten years the wheel would turn full circle and in that time thousands of holiday makers and day trippers would be forced away from the railway by savage cuts and closures, as the railways opted out of the seasonal market. Whilst we portray that the late 50s were the busiest time for excursions along the East Lancs. route, it is fair to say that by far the largest number of those excursion trains using the East Lancs. corridor to Preston and the Lancashire Coast, originated from Yorkshire starting points such as Hull, Leeds, Bradford, Batley, Wakefield and even Sheffield. The excursion trains from Yorkshire would of course join our route from Colne at Gannow Junction on the outskirts of Burnley, having just descended the incline from Copy Pit. The favourite seaside destination was of course Blackpool, but Morecambe and Southport also figured greatly for day trips out by rail. Half day excursions were by far the most popular and these would run at Easter and Whitsuntide and at weekends throughout the summer season. Period summer trains also ran to various holiday resorts allowing travel out and back over different weeks. Boat train specials would run to Liverpool, Heysham and Fleetwood, especially at the local holidays, connecting with sailings to Ireland and the Isle of Man. At the local holiday fortnight, a wide range of excursion services would run from Colne and Nelson, calling at stations along the East Lancs. route to Blackburn and whilst our journey to the seaside relates to the local resorts of Southport, Morecambe and Blackpool, there was a wide choice of destinations for local rail travellers in the late 1950s, when the holidays came around. The longer rail journeys included North Wales and the Cambrian Coast, the South Coast from Margate to Weymouth as well as the Isle of Wight, deepest Devon and Cornwall, and the East Coast resorts of Great Yarmouth, Filey and Scarborough. Strangely enough Scotland was much less catered for and it seemed that journeys up North tended to take the shape of very long day trips, to such places as Largs and Balloch Pier. In those busy excursion days by far the largest group of holidaymakers were the "Daytrippers", those who chose to stay at home, yet who wanted to visit the seaside or be it a variety of seaside destinations. Families such as ours, in common with many thousands of others from Colne, Nelson, Brierfield and Burnley etc. would purchase the ever popular Town Holiday Runabout Rover tickets, known to us simply as the "Runabouts". Believe me, the term runabout meant just that - certainly if our family was anything to go by. I wish that I had a £1 for every time that we've run up through the narrow streets (Bonnie Street etc.) close by Blackpool's Central station in an effort to catch our returning train to Colne. These tickets were exceptional value, in 1955, the 3rd class variety would set you back all of 26 shillings and sixpence, for six days unlimited travel over the given area of East and West Lancashire, bounded by Formby in the South, Wigan, Darwen, Colne and Barnoldswick heading East and Windermere and the Barrow Coast in the North. Unlimited journeys were also allowed on the Lake Windermere steamers. The price of the tickets altered little in the next few years; mind you neither did wages or prices in the shops. The price of the "Runabouts" had risen to 30 shillings for the 2nd class ticket by the holidays of 1962 (third class had by now of course been abolished). Despite the cheap price, the tickets always seemed to command a certain respect when offered at the many ticket barriers we passed through, possibly the rail staff felt a type of loyalty with the families who were prepared to spend their whole holidays hopping on and off trains. The slogan used in later advertisements read " The Runabout Rover, just the ticket for stay-at-home holidaymakers" and never was a more true statement made.....!
Growing up in the 1950s presented us with a mixture of post war austerity, old values and the high hopes of a bright new modern world in the 1960s, no wonder we were confused at times. There was still a lot of tradition and old ideals on the railways at this time. With regard to the excursion trains, little changed as the years rolled by. Each year you would see the same sights at the seaside stations such as Blackpool Central and Southport's Chapel Street etc. At Blackpool the two old ex.Lancashire and Yorkshire Barton Wright tank engines which sat between platforms Nos.6 and 7 (close by the toilet block) were firm favourites and we looked forward to pulling into the station besides them each year. Southport's station pilots Nos.50781 and 50746 were also old friends, their numbers would appear year after year in our spotting books. Somehow the security of seeing these familiar things still there year after year lulled us into believing that the magic of those happy summer days would never end, but as they say "All good things must come to an end" and for many of us the end came much to swiftly with the onset of the so-called swinging 60s
Of the three major Lancashire seaside resorts Blackpool was undoubtedly the "Jewel in the Crown". It had so much to offer the thousands of daytrippers who poured off the excursion trains at the Town's three main stations. The Central station was almost on the seafront - what more could you ask. Along the Golden Mile the sands stretched far to the South and way up to the North Shore. Three piers provided endless entertainment and side shows attractions and waxworks as well as cafés and tea bars etc. lined the seafront. The Blackpool Tower complex of ballrooms, circus and zoo was surrounded by theatres such as The Grand and The Palace as well as The Queens in Bank Hey Street, which had formerly been called Feldmans. Just behind there was The Winter Gardens Theatre and Ballroom. Woolworths slightly modern store dominated the area close by the Tower, the "Woolies" clock being as much a part of Blackpool as the tower itself. The cafeteria upstairs at Woolworths could seat 2000 people at any one time and a army of caterers would serve up meals with military

The Holiday Shutdown. Laithe Street in Colne 1958 and the streets are empty as the holiday fortnight begins. Thomas Foulds and Sons Ltd., Green shed is seen in the foreground and high on the hill sits the town of "Bonnie" Colne. Behind the camera a cinder path lead up the carriage sheds near the railway viaduct. *Stanley Duxbury.*

Brian Hyland.(seen left) gave us classic summer records at the dawn of the 1960s.

precision ....!

At its height the summer trade in rail travellers along the Fylde Coast reached 120,000 a day and as was pointed out earlier, up the coast at Fleetwood, thousands of holidaymakers could be seen heading off for the Isle of Man.

When we think of the seaside resorts all those years ago, it is hard not to recall the music of that era. How different it was from that of today. Over the years a number of famous records reached dizzy heights in July, which was the local Colne and Nelson holiday period. In 1955 whilst at the cinema we could watch the railway film "The Love Match", with Arthur Askey and Glenn Melvyn, we could also have seen him at Blackpool doing summer season together with Glenn and his own daughter Anthea. Local Preston man Eddie Calvert (The man with the golden trumpet) was meanwhile topping the charts with his version of "*Cherry Pink and Apple Blossom White*". Eddie was one of two major stars of show business who nearly always played the summer season at Blackpool, the other was of course the legendary Alma Cogan. From the early 1950s until 1962, she only missed doing the summer shows at Blackpool in 1958 and in that year , she was just up the coast at the Winter Gardens in Morecambe. Record hits at Colne holidays remembered from the seaside include, The Diamonds "*Little Darling*" in 1956, The King Bros. "*A White Sports Coat and Pink Carnation*" in 1957, The Mudlarks and "*Lollipop*" in 1958, Russ Conway (the resident pianist on the Billy Cotton Band show) was popular in July of 1959 with "*Roulette*" and by 1960 bikini fever was sweeping Britain and young Brian Hyland's catchy tune "*Itsy Bitsy Yellow Polka Dot Bikini*", was all the rage (I won't enlighten you as to the rude words we used as we sang along to this popular ditty). As you may recall many of those flimsy bikini's were made of lightweight Gingham cotton and once they became wet they left little to the imagination; its no wonder we were "*Halfway to Paradise*", as we listened to Billy Fury along the Blackpool seafront in the summer of 1961.

Enough of this frivolity, its now time for a look at just who the people were on those summer excursion trains of the 1950s. Life in milltown Lancashire and Colne was no exception, still revolved very much around the cotton industry. Whilst you could no longer say "England's bread hangs by Lancashire's thread", our lives were certainly still ruled by it. It was commonsense therefore to have a holiday fortnight when all the mills would take the same two weeks off, the period was known simply as The Colne, Nelson and District Holidays, unlike the mill areas of Rochdale, Shaw and Oldham etc, where the holidays tended to be called the "Wakes weeks". Engineering works and foundries also took the same holidays as much of their work was related to the cotton industry. It could be said therefore that in the 1950s, the local towns around Colne would simply shut down for two weeks at the beginning of July each year. The holidays always began on the first Saturday of July; Brierfield, Burnley, Hapton, Rose Grove and Padiham also took the same holiday fortnight and as you can imagine this meant a fair percentage of the many inhabitants of these local towns would be heading off to the Lancashire Coast resorts, be it to stay or just for the day. Earby and Barnoldswick near to Colne took the same holidays as Skipton for many years, before falling in line with Colne in the 1960s. When this happened connecting rail services ferried passengers to Earby and Colne so that they had access to the seaside specials. Skipton holidays incidentally were usually the middle two weeks in July. Accrington, Rishton, Great Harwood and the Blackburn area would normally take the last two weeks in July and as a rule all the coaching stock used at Colne holidays and stored at Colne would simply be called upon to cover the many special excursion trains operated in connection with the Blackburn holidays.

The start of the holidays would see the mills wind down. Most mills were still on the three shift system and leading up to the Friday night and Saturday morning of the holidays the millworkers would set out for home eager to finish packing, happy in the knowledge that work was over for a fortnight and with their "holidays with pay" tucked safely away, they would make ready for their departure by rail, either on the overnight Friday departures or on the early Saturday morning specials, and if they were only day tripping, then no doubt many would be celebrating in the pub.on Friday night. Many would be seen picking up leaflets and buying tickets at Colne station, which was a

(above and lower right) **In the Mill.** Happy weavers look forward to their annual break, left to right are Dorothy Ibbotson, Florrie Broughton, Edna Bottomley and Margaret Rushton, lower right we see Edna Heap making warps in the preparation dept., during the summer of 1958. *Stanley Duxbury.*

(below) **Jimmy Heap.** Dad's old pal Jimmy Heap was very much a working mill manager at Foulds Green shed mill, everybody pulled together in those days, Jimmy's main helper at the time was one Tommy Haythornthwaite a true Lancashire character who had everyone in stitches with his humour. *Jimmy Heap.*

hive of activity on the eve of the holidays. On the whole most of us used the trains at that time, those that chose to go by road for their holidays would stand in draughty Albert Road near the Ribble offices and then face a cramped ride in a 29 seater Bedford model **'O'** coach or maybe they'd be lucky enough to ride in one of the later Burlingham "Seagull" coaches used by both Ribble and Standerwick. Whatever the case they were no match for the railways, but how soon would this change in just a few short years. The clatter of the looms would cease and the mill boilers would have their fires drawn. For once the tall blackened mill chimneys would cease to smoke. So much clearer was the air around Colne that even Pendle Hill some miles from Colne, would stand out twice as sharp in the clear summer sunshine. The old cart road wending its way up the side of Pendle Hill would be easily seen from Colne's railway station. In order to finance the annual break away, the millworkers would join their mill holiday club. This was usually run by a member of the office staff in the wages department. Millworkers having opened their wage packets would then pay into the club the amounts they needed to fund their holiday requirements. As the holiday approached, the sums of money were paid out to the club members upon production of their holiday club cards. Most firms ran a club. Even the railway did, and you may recall the loss of the holiday fund money formed the major part of the story surrounding Arthur Askey and Glenn Melvyn' s film, *The Love Match*. Occasionally the temptation to run off with the holiday club money became too great and one or two wages clerks have been known to have absconded with the "lolly", only to return to face the music at a later stage. Rather them than me. The thought of facing a load of angry women weavers wielding shuttles and wearing clogs would be too much .....!

Many of the mills in our area in the 50s would employ anything from 50 to 500 workers or so, but a few little family-type weaving sheds could still be seen and it was often these small units which would outlive the big boys by many years, as we entered the 1960s. Just like the documentaries seen on the telly that portrayed Lancashire life, showing the deserted streets with dogs howling, an eery silence would prevail around the streets close by the weaving sheds. In later years as the cotton industry faded away, that eery silence on the streets was not just confined to the holiday period. The excitement leading up to those last few days that marked the start of the local holidays will I feel, never be forgotten, it really was the highlight of the year.

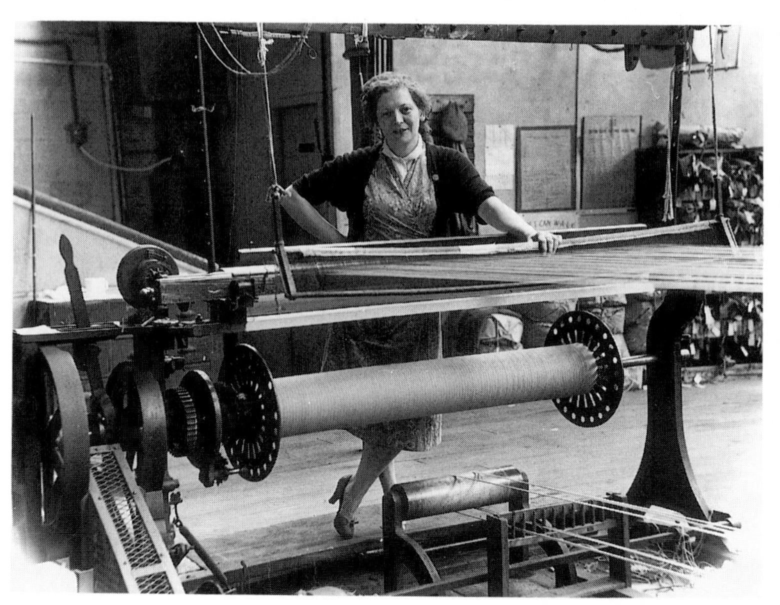

The start of the holidays.

As other local people dashed about with suitcases etc. on the Friday night and Saturday morning at the start of the local holidays, we would have to contain our excitement at least until Sunday, for this was the first day of the "Runabout" ticket. Therefore we rarely became involved in the hectic happenings down at the railway station that took place as the holidays got under way. Dad would still be working in his capacity as boilerman and engineer at Thomas Mason's which was a biggish textile mill that was visible from the railway at Primet Hill. It would be dad's job the wind things down and in effect close the mill up for the holidays. Occasionally in the late 1950s we would go down on that Saturday morning at the start of the holiday to help dad shut every thing down, after which the plan was usually to walk up to the railway station and collect the "Runabout" tickets ready for the week's day-trips that lay ahead. Dad would have been at the mill since 5am, which was normal. Bert and I would have quietly strolled down about 11am and our journey would have taken us around by Green Road and Knotts Lane which passed under the railway viaduct, the seaside specials would be seen backing into the station one by one and departing, high above us across the high arched viaduct. Already the streets were quiet and you could really sense the atmosphere of the holidays. It felt grand and there was a feeling of excitement as we made our way through the streets, the bright summer sun felt warm on our backs and soon we were discarding our jackets as the morning heated up. Up on the carriage sidings, high on the banking to the left of us, the sound of engine whistles and steam blowing impatiently from the locos. safety valves filled the air as the engines shunted their trains about and prepared for the journey ahead. There was little road traffic to prevent us crossing the normally busy main road at the bottom of Primet Hill. Soon we were in the dark confines of Primet Mill, round by the boiler, the heat was well into the 90s. Dad would greet us with a surprised look and would try to act as though he hadn't expected to see us down at the mill, when really mum had probably told him the night before that we were planning to go with him to pick up the tickets from the station. Taking his hanky out to wipe the sweat from his neck and forehead, he'd voice the opinion "Shouldn't be too long now,". The mill was already reasonably quiet and we had to pass by most of the weaving sheds to gain access to the boiler room, the various workers were already washing off and preparing for home as dinnertime approached. Round at the boiler dad had shut the fires down. Masons Mill had converted to oil fired boilers in 1947 and the boiler fuel consisted of heavy black treacle-like oil which needed to be kept warm and passed through a preheater in order to be the right viscosity to be forced at speed into the firehole via a firing pin which resembled a steel hammer. We'd help dad clean and store the firing pins, close the dampers and shut down the little steam pumps for oil and water. We'd then go up in the spotless engine house where the giant flywheel was still revolving. Dad as a rule would let one of us bring the huge wheel to a stand by operating the governor that controlled the speed and operation of the power plant. The engine room would fall silent, only the ticking of the engine house clock could then be heard. This clock retained in a glass cabinet had a large brass bell push which acted as a clocking in system and like everyone else in those days, dad would clock in and out. The steam in the boiler was blown down and out in to the river behind the mill, and whilst watching this process we could look up through the mills where high above on the railway viaduct the many excursion trains continued to depart on their seaside trips. Sadly we were too far away to be able to note the engine numbers of the various locos. as they passed to and fro. Soon dad would put on his cap and coat and we would switch out the many lights before pulling the white

Round by the Boiler: Dad is carefully monitoring the oil flow to the boilers at Thomas Masons Primet mill.The Clyde burners are brightly burning as the twin spy holes show. My first attempts at steam raising were on these very boilers. *S. Taylor.*

Colne Station Frontage. As the holidays got under way the station forecourt would be full of holidaymakers preparing to head off into the sun for a week or two. *Michael Feather.*

washed boilerhouse doors together and locking them. We would head out of the mill closing doors and switching off the lights as we went. Finally the mill gate would be closed and firmly bolted. Now it really was the start of the holidays.

On the short winding walk up Primet Hill to the railway station we became aware once more of the many departing special trains. As we headed past the coal shutes and under the railway overbridge, yet another special rumbled high above us, and we often wondered was that a Llandudno or just another Blackpool-bound relief train. Climbing up the stone staircase to the station yard, the scene was one of apparent chaos, with a mass of people all waiting, suitcases in hand to either use the subway or purchase tickets. Dad would join the queue in order to purchase the "Runabout" tickets and meanwhile Bert and myself would watch with great interest the madcap happenings as these local holidaymakers dashed about and panicked in fear of missing their seaside specials. On the various blackboards that lined the station entrance one of the more artistic members of the staff had neatly listed all the holiday specials in a colourful array of chalks. Judging by the fancy lettering and style, this persons talent was obviously wasted portering at Colne. Eventually dad staggered out of the booking hall area, its bare wooden floor resounding to the many pairs of feet now passing though it, in his hand he clutched a pile of leaflets and handbills relating to the holiday trains "C'mon let's be going" he'd shout with the urgency of a bomber pilot who, having dropped his load, was anxious to depart the scene before being shot down. We would quickly head away past the many holidaymakers that were still rolling up for the seaside specials, out across the station yard and down Bridge Street, before wending our way via the long straight road which lead to Waterside and our home. As we walked along dad was already scanning the leaflets and making comparisons with previous years, pointing out that there was as usual little change in the

holiday trains that we would be using. Looking back over my shoulder I could see yet another holiday special setting out over the viaduct, whistling as it departed, now the excitement was really mounting. Come the morning we too would be heading out over that very same viaduct; ahead of us would lie a very hectic week, riding on the seaside specials from East Lancashire.

Planning the Day Trips by Excursion Train.

The day to day schedule for our seasonal day trips by train varied little over the years from 1952 until 1962. The week would begin on the Sunday as this was the first day of the Town Holiday Runabout ticket and as a rule we would begin our holidays with a leisurely look at Blackpool, making one of our odd trips to the Tower circus to see Charlie Cairoli. Usually we'd make at least two visits to the circus each year, possibly the other occasion would be when we visited the resort to see the illuminations in the autumn, always known to us as "going to see the lights". As a rule, Monday would see us taking a trip to Southport, travelling via the East Lancs. route to Bamber Bridge and then along the West Lancs. line via Hesketh Bank to Southport's St. Lukes and Chapel Street stations. Whilst the run to Southport was a pleasant change, the town itself was something of a culture shock in comparison with Blackpool and for some reason we never fully considered it as a proper seaside resort. Maybe this was because we never saw the sea at Southport, only miles and miles of sand. Tuesday was always a run to Morecambe as this was the local market day and after the usual journey to Preston we would travel out on the West Coast main line to Lancaster and then branch away to the left at Morecambe South Junction to reach Morecambe's Euston Road station, a place which was very handy for the markets and the local cafés. Wednesday would see us heading off up towards the Lake District to Lakeside station for a ride on the Windermere steamers. This was a trip always referred to by dad as going to "the Lakes". We would transfer straight onto the steamers at the Lakeside pier and after cruising the lake, we would make our way up to Windermere for tea before rejoining our return excursion train at the nearby station of Windermere Town. Our empty train had travelled round from Lakeside station by way of the loop line from Arnside to Hincaster Junction and then up to Oxenholme before running along the branch to Windermere. Thursday was another trip to Blackpool and as always we would arrive at the Central station there. Up to four specials would usually run to Blackpool each morning at the local holidays starting at either Skipton, Earby or Colne, at times varying from 8.30 am to 11.30 am. We would have no doubt had dinner at the large "Woolies" café adjacent to the Central station at Blackpool, followed by a relaxing hour or two on the very crowded beach close by the tower. Tea was often taken at the famous Foxhall Café in Foxhall Square, after which we would take a leisurely look at the back street shops (and there were many!) en-route to the station We would make our way up the narrow alley known as Bonnie Street, passing the railings close by the Number One platform at the Central station where often one of the tank engines on pilot duties would be seen simmering away. We would head for home as the sun began to fade.

Friday, our last trip of the week would again see us heading for Blackpool, but this time we'd go up north looking at Littlewoods store and Abingdon Street market en-route, and we would take a journey on the Fleetwood shuttle train from Blackpool North, powered by one of the little Stanier class 3 tanks such as Nos.**40109** or **40164** or the later Standard 84000 engines. The journey to Fleetwood was again a bit of a novelty, whilst being a short run via the Poulton Curve it was nevertheless interesting being a mixture of countryside and industry followed by a busy fishing port and ferry terminal. There was a lot to see and often many engines to "spot". The journey back to Blackpool was sometimes by train but more often than not a tram ride was taken right through to the South Shore. After an early tea and an odd hour on the Pleasure Beach we would make the final trip up to the Central station by way of the seafront and the back streets, making our departure back to Colne as late as possible on this last day trip.

On the odd occasion in the 1950s our family finances must have been looking up because now and again we would spend both our holiday weeks travelling to the Lancashire Coast resorts, though I do recall that we wouldn't use all the six days available as mum and dad liked a odd days break at home before going back to work.

Along Shaw Road. Always known to us as Shaw Road, but it was in fact called Shaw Street. This long almost straight road, ran all the way from Waterside where we lived, to Bridge Street which was close to the station. From this point half way along its length we had a good view of the viaduct and of the trains reversing in and setting off. *S. Taylor.*

Heading for the station.

The Sunday of Colne's annual holidays would start bright and early for us and I would assist mum packing bags, sorting food out and filling flasks, brother Bert on the other hand would be out with dad making sure all the animals on the small-holding we had were fed and watered. Dad kept a large number of hens and as a rule our sandwiches on these day trips tendered always to be a bit on the "eggy" side. Once the flasks were filled etc. we would set off for the station leaving dad and Bert to follow us when the animals had been watered. As we headed out along Waterside and Shaw Road, (the long straight road leading to the station), we would take worried glances back through "Damside" to see if dad and Bert had set off. Along Shaw Road at this time stood Shaw Mills, owned by scrap merchants, George Rushworth and Sons. This large mill complex with its tall main building and extensive weaving sheds had become the storage point for hundreds of tons of scrap loom parts as the local mills began closing one after another in the post war era. Rushworths famous scrap pile of Lancashire looms was a dominant feature of Colne's south valley and this huge high pile of scrap was easily seen from the railway viaduct. It was a constant reminder to local people of what the future had in store for this little weaving community of ours. As we passed by Rushworths scrapyard, we would see the various excursion trains setting back over the viaduct from the carriage sheds to the station at Colne, the bright morning sunlight glinted off the varnished coach sides as they gently reversed across the six arch viaduct. At the end of Shaw Road was Bridge Street, on the corner there close by the station we would look back along Shaw Road usually spotting dad and Bert as they came out of the shadow of Shaw Mills and into the sunlight. Dad as always would be wearing his light grey suit with the familiar cardigan beneath it and one of those silky ties so popular in the 50s.

He would be striding out vigorously and more often than not, he would have one hand in his pocket, meanwhile brother Bert would be hard pressed to keep pace with him. Re-assured that they were coming, we'd cross the then quiet main road and join the crowds of day trippers who were now converging upon the station yard from all parts of Colne, the feeling was something akin to the scene in the Ealing studios film The Titfield Thunderbolt, where the crowds are seen making their way down the village lane to board the train to Mallingford. There was noise and laughter in the air as we made our way down the winding subway slope, shafts of sunlight lit the normally dark damp tunnel and as always the smell of damp and coal gas was ever present. At the subway bottom, a staircase on the right led up to the platform above, it was from this platform that all our seaside journeys began. The subway continued under the two main lines and on the far wall of the subway was a large red enamel sign declaring that trains to Skipton and beyond departed from the platform above. Sometimes as we reached the bottom of the stone stair case leading up to our departure platform, a loud rumble above the girders would indicate to us that yet another special was backing into the station. This approaching train would make us hurry all the more in case this one was ours. More often than not though by the time we climbed the stairs our service to the seaside had not yet backed up from the sidings.

We always stood round the corner from the subway, near the platform slope, it was here that a large bell was mounted to the subway wall and this acted as a warning system to platform staff of passing trains, with both lines capable of having trains operating in both directions (many of them propelling), it was a much appreciated safety factor for the platform staff. The majority of people seemed to congregate to-

Primet Hill. To the left of the picture is Bridge Street and Shaw Road. the station yard is on the right and Colne's 6 arched viaduct is out of sight behind the local barbers shop of Stanley Hendleys. *Don Speak.*

gether in the middle of the platform, all would be busily in conversation, laughter filled the air and there was an intense sense of excitement on the crowded platform. The large bell would ring and dad would pipe up "That's ours coming now"! and sure enough the plume of smoke rising over at the carriage sheds beyond the viaduct indicated to us which of the many sets of coaching stock seen in the distance was to be our train that day. Slowly the brake-van of the reversing train would snake out along the viaduct towards us, somewhat further in the distance, little clouds of smoke would rise with every puff of the locomotive that was powering our seaside special. As the train came nearer we could see the two rear windows in the non - corridor brake-van and as a rule the train reporting number was pasted up in one of the windows, **C 882** for example, or in later years **1T52.** The guard could be seen leaning out carefully monitoring events as the train set back to the platform. With the brake-van about to enter the platform, the porters would begin to call out the trains destination. "Blackpool Central .... Blackpool train" was the cry which went up more often than not. As many as four or five Blackpools' would depart Colne on certain dates at the holidays. The coaches of the excursion train would roll steadily into the platform with a resounding thud as they passed over the rail joints, the sunlit platform would suddenly go dark as the coaches blotted out the bright sunlight. The waiting crowd on the platform looked anxiously at the empty compartments flashing past them, ready to make a mad scramble for seats as the special came to rest. The reasonably short platforms at Colne would only hold 6 coaches at the most and therefore at least the three rear vehicles would be some distance beyond the platform, out towards Colne North signalbox. The loco. at the head of the train would come to a stand at the platform end , its wheels and motion grinding slowly to a halt by the ornate Midland Railway water column. The loco. crew would be seen looking back eagerly watching the mad dash for seats. As always dad made a beeline for the first compartment behind the engine. There were distinct advantages to riding here, as normally the leading compartment was all but drawn off the platforms at the stations en-route and the waiting crowds in their eagerness for seats would not bother to run all the way to the front hoping for an empty compartment. The only main disadvantage was that being so close to the tender etc. if you had the window open you were covered in coal dust as well as smoke from the engine, this could get worse if the boiler for instance was over filled and all too often we ended up arriving at Blackpool looking like at set of touring black and white minstrels. This problem with the grime could have been sorted out before we reached the coast had we leaned out passing Lea Road troughs, then we'd have received a free shower courtesy of the engine crew.

Having got tucked into the roomy surroundings of our non-corridor compartment, dad would drop the window and lean out, his large frame filled the carriage window and helped deter any would-be boarders. We in turn would press ourselves against the windows in an effort to make the compartment look full. That first trip of the holidays felt great, here you were back again raring to go, the familiar surroundings of the compartment made it feel like you were home once more, it gave you a sort of reassurance that in the last twelve months nothing had changed. The hard horsehair seats still made the same groaning sounds as you bounced on the springs sending a cloud of dust up from their Paisley patterned material covers. The smell of fresh varnish was ever present and there was always a generous amount of it applied to the window sills where the condensation usually gathered. Up on the compartment walls would be the usual three pictures a side depicting either seaside resorts or the Lake District and just occasionally a few of the more ornate coaches would have pictures of Victorian trains instead of the normal scenic views of the Lancashire Coast.

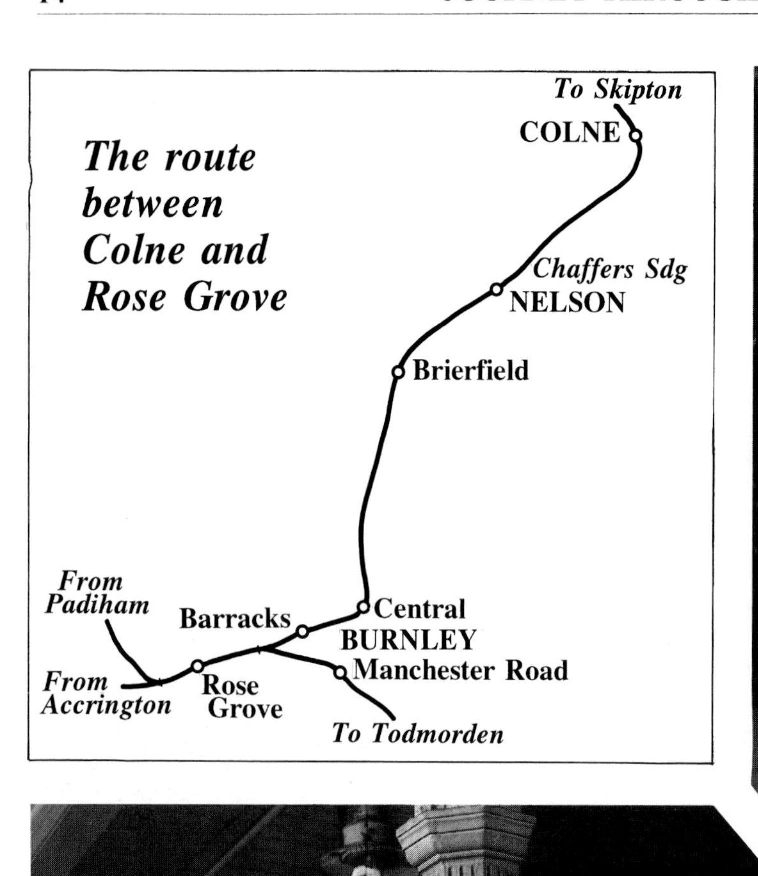

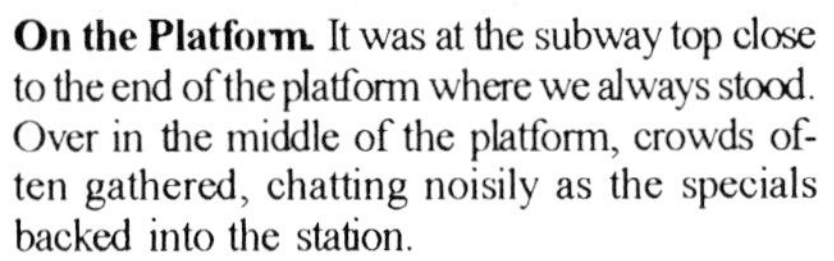

On the Platform. It was at the subway top close to the end of the platform where we always stood. Over in the middle of the platform, crowds often gathered, chatting noisily as the specials backed into the station.
S.Taylor /Tim Proctor Colne Times newspaper.

View Across the Viaduct. As we stood by the subway top, anxiously looking out across the viaduct towards the carriage sheds, the large bell near us would warn of an incoming train.Accrington's No.**75049** slips quietly into the platform with a local service on 17th July 1955. *Colin Boocock.*

All Aboard. Tucked in the comfy non-corridor compartment, these lads seen here on the right look full of excitement at the prospect of a seaside trip.The partition walls of the compartments of these non-corridor coaches usually featured three pictures per side. *S.Taylor.*

Setting out.
Moving onto the viaduct we were treated to some excellent views of the south valley right up towards Carry Bridge. In the foreground down below us is Colne Water and the bottom of Knotts Lane. (Below),coming off the viaduct we would pass the carriage sidings, here No.**42734** shunts stock into the sidings.
S.Taylor / Stuart James.

The journey begins....... Colne to Rose Grove.

The loco. whistle would sound and dad would turn his head into the compartment to say "That's us.....we're off", with nobody riding with us we had the run of the compartment and as we edged out over the high viaduct we manned both the open carriage windows eagerly enjoying the privileged view, as always I was only too aware that many of my school mates wouldn't even be getting one day trip let alone a weeks train rides. As the train slipped quietly over the viaduct towards the carriage sheds, our gaze often followed the line of the river below and we would be looking out towards Knotts Lane bottoms and the gas works yard and far beyond over to Waterside where we lived, the cows grazing in farmer Roy Smiths fields at Pike Laithe farm close to where we lived could easily been seen even at such a long distance. (This farm high on the hillside of the valley is where the wooden carriage shed buildings now sit, having been removed to there in 1968).

The busy carriage sheds now appeared on our left side, whilst over on the right the later 1913 excursion sidings held yet more specials lined up ready to back up to the station. The shunters cabin stood at the Laithe Street end of the carriage sheds and sometimes the shunting staff such as Norman Fishwick and Frank Bairstow would be seen having a break sat near the little mess hut. Passing the wooden structure of the carriage sheds we could clearly see through the gap in the boards on the shed side just how big an area these sheds covered. There were six covered sidings all with wooden walkways and the first road in the shed up to the main line had a really long inspection pit, apparently this is where the London stock was kept, this siding always being kept clear for the last London arrival late at night.

Just before the local holidays in July 1959, a new staff amenity block had been completed close by the Nelson end of the carriage sidings at Wackersall Bridge, the opening of this red bricked facility coincided with the opening of the new Roman Catholic School of Fisher More, which was situated just a few fields away from the carriage sheds. The school had opened in May of 1959 but the playing fields down by the railway line were still being laid out in July of that year. The clatter of pointwork and the passing of Wackersall Bridge itself signified the end of the carriage sheds and the approach to Colne's No. 1 signalbox, behind which lay another school , the much older Primet Secondary Modern, which was also of red brick.

Only a short distance lay between Colne No.1 and the Colne-Nelson boundary. Here, close by the boundary field was the little railway halt of Bott Lane, sometimes called Bott House Lane after the little lane which ran up to the railway from the main road. The tiny halt consisted of just a sleepered area and a wooden waiting hut. Nearby was the Hollins housing estate, better known to us in the 1950s as "Chinatown" , this was due to the fact the estate had been built of Prefabs, the tiny garden shed type housing that had been created in post war times to help the housing shortage. At night these quaint little houses could be seen illuminated by the curiously white sodium street lamps dotted around the estate. The white street lighting in Nelson was most unusual as most East Lancashire towns had the more normal yellow or orange lighting. In the evening light as you approached Nelson a sort of whitish blue glow could be seen in the night sky such was the good quality of Nelson's street lighting and it must be said that the lighting was the best of any town locally.

Colne Carriage Sheds. Slipping quietly out of Colne past the carriage sheds gave us ample chance to view the other excursion trains as they waited to back up to the station. Rows of coaching stock filled both sides of the railway at this point. *Stuart James.*

The Colne Times, Fri., July 1, 1955.

Your Holiday Requirements

All Home Perms, Face Cloths, Bathing Caps, Toilet Holdalls, Thermos Flasks, Drinking Cups, Films, Kodak Cameras from 24/6

obtainable at

COLNE CO-OP. CHEMISTS, 32 CHURCH STREET

Colne Wackersall Bridge 15.6.63. At the Nelson end of the carriage sidings looking back towards Colne, we see No.**75032** departing on its journey to Southport at 11.16am, a regular Saturdays only working. In the downside excursion sidings behind 75032, is No.**61024** with Blackpool special 1T52. *Brian Wrigglesworth.*

Bott Lane Halt. This little halt situated at the Colne Nelson boundary, was served by the railmotor "Puffing Billy" service until December 1956. The post war "Prefabs" mentioned in the text are seen behind the halt. We always called this housing estate "China town". The white glow of the street lamps there at night helped all the more to give the area an oriental feel. *Michael Feather*

Capture your holiday memories in GLORIOUS COLOUR with an easy-to-use

KODAK INSTAMATIC 100

Takes sparkling colour slides, colour prints or black and white.

ONLY £5-4-8

With built-in flash gun.

Let us show you the KODAK Still and Movie range.

H. B. TONKS M.P.S.

359, LEEDS ROAD (Boundary), NELSON

Nelson Mineral Yard.

Beyond the boundary , the large expanse of Nelson's Mineral Yard opened up to reveal a vast number of sidings containing dozens of coal wagons, mountains of coal and even the odd row or two of coaching stock over near the back sidings. Speed would fall at this point as we drew up to the home signal relating to Chaffers Sidings. Below the railway banking here was Hallam Road, along which a number of large cotton mills were situated. We had now begun to catch up the preceding excursions and we would crawl up to Chaffers inner home signal, to await the excursion in front loading passengers at Nelson Station. Two high latticed footbridges spanned the railway at Chaffers, one close to the Co-op abattoir and the other next to the level crossing itself, both these vantage points were popular with trainspotters and kids alike, especially at the holiday periods. When our turn came to load passengers at Nelson station, we would drift quietly over the level crossing at Chaffers and run past the famous Victory “V” lozenges factory of Messrs. Fryer and Co; a small firm with a big turnover, they were very famous for the cough sweets, but it is not commonly known that their biggest selling item was jelly babies. Literally millions of these kiddies favourites were produced over the years at the former textile mill close to Nelsons town centre and even at the local holidays it was business as usual as far as Victory ”V“ was concerned.

Colne Nelson Boundary. Black 5 No.**45388** hurries along towards Mineral Sidings coal yard near to the boundary field.The large building to the top left is the Nelson Grammer School and always seen on the skyline at this point was the spire of St Mary’s church.
Eddie Bobrowski

Mineral Sidings. The signal box seen here to the right controlled entry to the large coal yard at Mineral Sidings in Nelson. The sidings themselves were beyond the overbridge in the background (Walton Lane). Black 5 No.**45227** heads for Colne with a parcels train on a bright sunny morning.
Bill Hurst

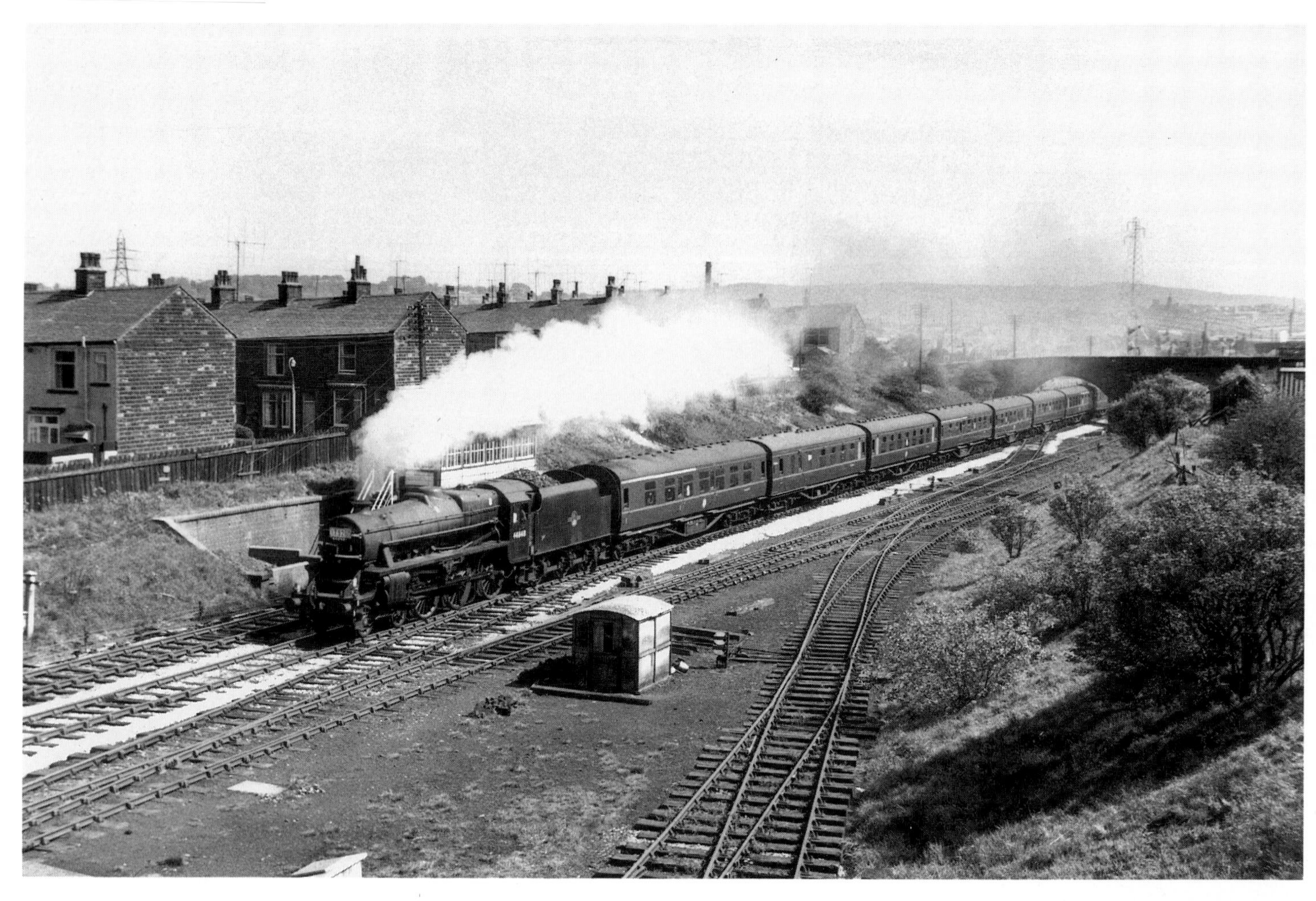

10.45am to Windermere 29.5.66. No.**44848** speeds past Mineral Sidings in this view taken from Walton Lane bridge. Colne can be seen over to the right above the overbridge.
Stuart James.

Chaffers Siding Cabin. We would often wait here until a preceding excursion had loaded passengers at Nelson station, just round the bend. This little cabin controlled the busy Barkerhouse Road level crossing, seen just to the right of the signalbox. Over on the left is a picture of well known Chaffers signalman Wilf King.
S.Taylor / Bill Hurst.

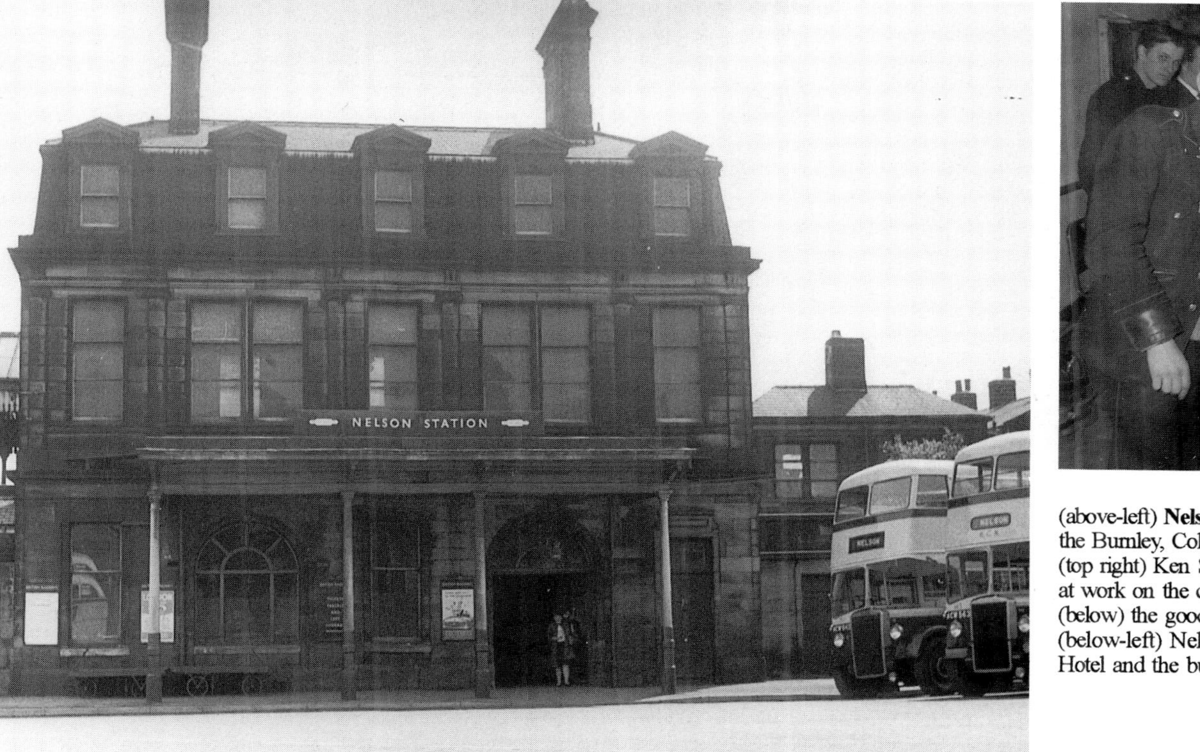

(above-left) **Nelson Station.** the main station building frontage, with the Burnley, Colne & Nelson buses to the right.
(top right) Ken Stout and Michael Greenwood, (seen on the left) are at work on the club layout in their premises at 33 Vine Street.
(below) the goods warehouse as seen from the platform.
(below-left) Nelson station signalbox, behind which is the Station Hotel and the bus stabling point.

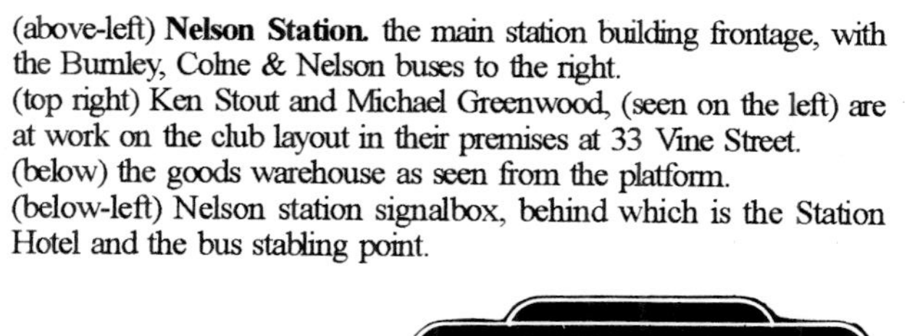

Nelson station.

Round the bend from the red bricked lozenge factory of Victory "V", the island platform of Nelson station came into view, already our first glimpse of the station told us that the platform was heaving and as we rolled across Sagar Street viaduct nearing the platform edge you could see the tense crowd getting ready to storm the train once we came to rest. The station at Nelson was always well patronised being right in the centre of town. The railway travelled through the town centre high on an embankment for most of the way and rolling through the left side of the island platform, we could see the gable ends of the many rundown terraced houses that were situated next to the railway at this point. Rows and rows of terraced accommodation filled the dozens of streets that stretched up the hillside to our left. Even further left a wide array of mill chimneys rose high above the rooftops, this area was known as Valley Mills.

A main thoroughfare ran beneath the middle of the platform, this in the 1950s was the then thriving shopping area of Railway Street, always very busy indeed. Just up Railway Street, No.57 in fact, a gentleman named Ken ran a very successful model railway business for many years.

The speed of our excursion train as we ran through the platform was usually quite fast and we would pass the anxiously waiting crowd too quickly to register anyone we may have known. With a rumble of brakes we ground to a jerky halt at the platform end. Looking back down the train, a handful of the more energetic daytrippers were heading our way, it really was a case of fingers crossed here. As a rule they nearly always at this early stage in the journey were able to find spare compartments before they reached us. Soon, arms were being waved by the platform staff, giving a circling movement away from their body meant a move up was needed and with a pop on the whistle and a hiss from the engine's drain cocks we eased forward the odd carriage length to allow the rearmost coaches to enter the platform. By now we were standing near the subway of Hibson Road close to the small cattle dock, which by the late 1950s would see little use. Over on the right the large goods yard with its sizeable goods warehouse could be seen. Beneath the awning of the warehouse were stabled a number of Scammell trailers and no doubt nearby would be one or two of the familiar Scammell tractor units loading up ready for another local parcel delivery.

Nelson station goods yard also handled large amounts of coal traffic, even though the Mineral sidings were just across town. The station goods yard also had a travelling crane system situated over to the back side where the long sidings stretched out behind the goods warehouse.

Frantic whistling heralded our departure from Nelson station and with a deep hoot from the whistle our loco would steadily gather its train together and amble off past the goods yard on our right and head out of Nelson along the Hard Platts. This was the long straight section leading to Brierfield. With parkland to the left and the main Manchester road below us to the right, our train would be striding happily along , the driver hanging on the whistle as we passed the many foot crossings on this section of line.

A deep cutting and a left hand curve was followed by the short Brierfield tunnel. Our driver would shut off steam here and allow the loco to coast the short distance into Brierfield. Once through the blackened tunnel which ran beneath the main road to Burnley, we could see the tightly curved spur into the gas works there, which branched away to the right and beyond this point a tiny ground frame cabin operated the little sidings behind the down platform at Brierfield. There always seemed to be some of the petrol blue ICI tank wagons stabled here. Dominating the area adjacent to the station was the huge mill premises owned by Messrs. Smith and Nephew Textiles Ltd., the large stone office frontage of the Brierfield Mills was and still is quite impressive, even in the 1950s neon illuminated letters were mounted high on the roof and at night the words Smith and Nephew could be seen a long way off.

(above) **Nelson Station.** The platform staff check the excursion list in readiness for the arrival of the holiday crowds and below we see the crowded upside platform at Nelson station, clearly still busy in the 1960s.

Barry Atkinson /Tim ProctorLeader/Times newspapers

Nelson Station. The frontage of the building was quite impressive, even the bathroom suite in the upstairs rooms was a deep shade of blue with inlaid patterns and fancy ornamental taps. Access to the trains was via the booking hall where a ramp led up to the platform above.Burnley Colne and Nelson Joint Transport buses were stabled for many years in the station yard, over at the right hand side. Bus drivers Ken Stout, Harold Eccles and Alan Catlow joined David Carter Michael Greenwood and John Porter and others in forming the Brierfield Model Railway Club in 1964 and this club would be the last resident of the rather unique station building at Nelson.

The pictures here are by *David Carter (1) and E. Blakey (courtesy of the L and Y Soc.,) (3).*

(below) The Windermere special seen earlier at Mineral Sidings is now departing from Nelson, note the Victory "**V**" factory close to Chaffers Siding Cabin, seen here behind the station building in the middle distance. *Stuart James.*

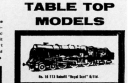

On the Platform. Running into the upside platform at Nelson, we would pass close by the gable ends of the somewhat shabby terraced houses that stood next to the railway line. These gable ends were painted with adverts for the local building societies and the Nelson Leader newspaper. Railway Street ran beneath the station at this point.
G.H.Platt.

(No. 2) (No. 2)
2nd- CHEAP SINGLE CHEAP SINGLE -2nd
Burnley (Central) to
Burnley (Central) Nelson Burnley (Central) Nelson
NELSON
(M) 0/7 Fare 0/7 (M)
For conditions see over conditions see over
6800 6800

Awaiting the "Tip". On a warm sunny morning, this seaside special prepares to leave for the coast. The fireman, oblivious of the engine's smoky chimney looks hard through the bright sunlight trying to catch the "tip" from the platform staff at Nelson. Eager young faces excitedly look out of the carriage windows. *Ken Stout.*

Brierfield Tunnel. The view here is from the loading dock close by the gasworks entrance, looking in the Nelson direction back towards the "Hardplatts". The main road from Nelson to Burnley passed above the tunnel. Brierfield station was just a short distance away behind the camera. *E. Blakey, (courtesy of the L and Y Soc.,)*

BRIERFIELD

Brierfield Station (towards Nelson). No.**42187** coasts through the Up side platform at Brierfield and is about to rattle over the level crossing at the platform end (behind the camera). In the distance the line curves away to the right at Brierfield tunnel, as it heads towards Nelson. *Peter E. Baughan.*

DMU days. This picture of Brierfield is from the green painted footbridge which spanned the railway at this point. Looking in the Burnley direction as one of the new Accrington DMU 's enters the Platform in 1960. In the background we see the Brierfield Goods signalbox close to King Street Terrace. *John E Porter.*

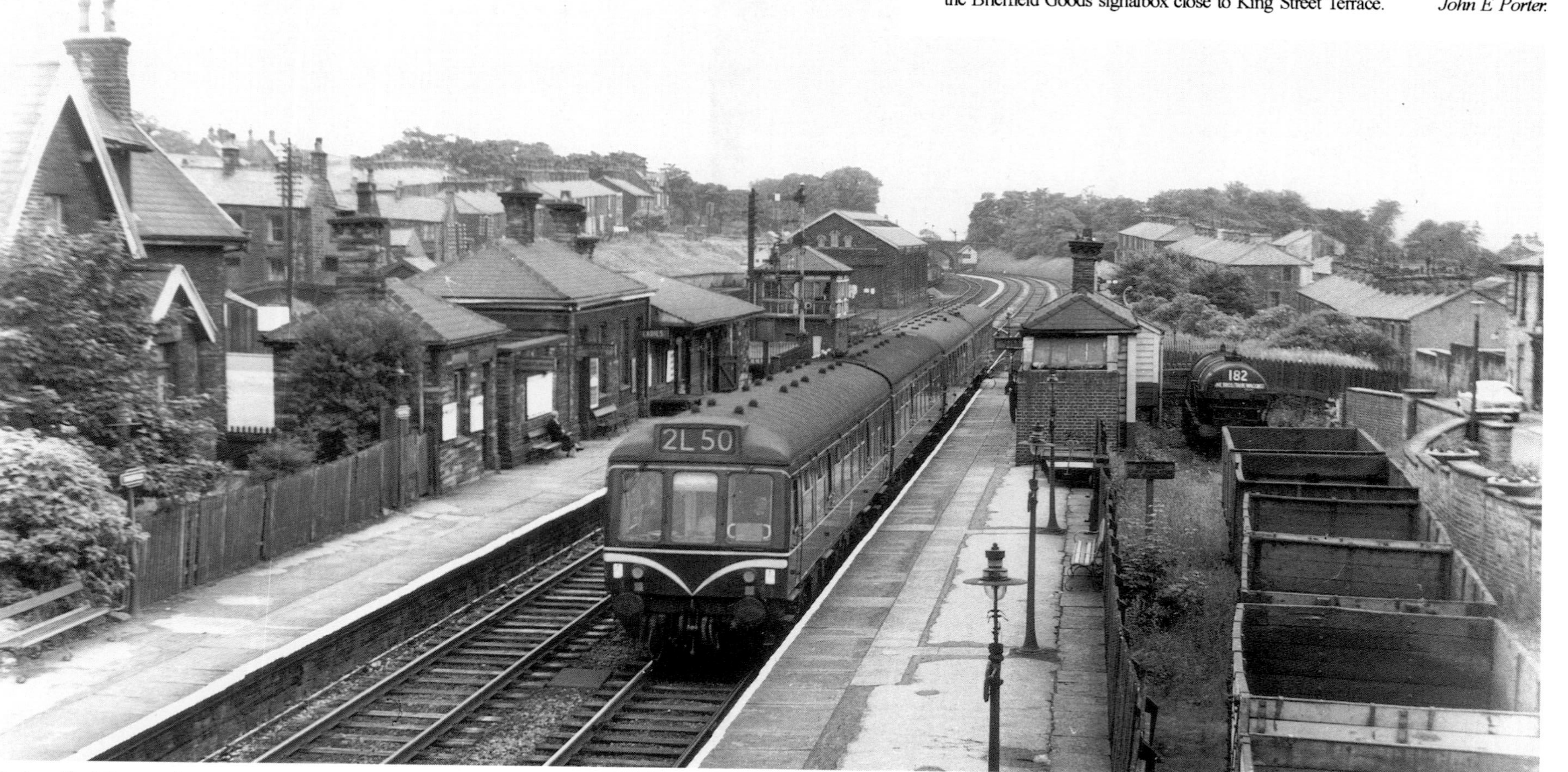

Brierfield station.

Brierfield station buildings resembled very much those of a rural country station, and it was only the grime from the mills that spoiled this impression. Both the up and down platforms would hold in the region of 8 coaches, even so we would more than likely draw up here as well.

The station buildings were of dressed stone on the upside platform, where a booking hall parcels office and waiting facilities were all provided as well as toilets. The down side buildings were a solid wood affair traditionally "Lanky" in design, they were now painted in the familiar red and cream colour scheme, with the red applied to the portion below the windows and the cream painted above. The impression of a country station was further enhanced by the large amount of market garden produce that was often piled high on the up platform by the ticket office. a number of local growers situated up the Halifax road area of the town would send much of their produce by rail and in view of the freshness factor, the majority of these items went by passenger services. From the platform at Brierfield you had a lovely view over the hills to Pendleside. At the platform end was a level crossing controlled by a typically "Lanky Camel" signalbox which was positioned on our left side. Over beyond the signalbox, lay the goods warehouse and like Nelsons, it too was built of dressed stone with a blue slate roof. A quite busy coal yard covered the area between the goods shed and the signalbox at the crossing, another signal cabin situated down at the far end of the goods yard, in the Burnley direction was positioned close to the overbridge at Massey Street. This signal cabin was known as Brierfield Goods. Also at the level crossing were two well known drinking establishments, namely The Railway Hotel and The Leeds and Liverpool. Heading away from the platform we would run past the goods yard on the left and over on the right below us down the embankment stood the slightly posh houses of King Street Terrace. Passing under Massey Street Bridge, we would clatter over the pointwork that led into the goods yard.

(top left) **Brierfield Station.** The large sign seen here was situated near to the subway on the Down side of the line at Brierfield station (Colne platform).The platform building on the Down side was a very solid wooden affair as we see opposite. The Up side buildings were more substantial, being of dressed stone. In the above picture a retirement presentation is taking place on the Up side platform, to the left of the group is Cyril Standaloft a familar fiqure in local booking offices for many years.

Mr. and Mrs. Standaloft.

Boat Train. 1K48 a Colne to Liverpool Exchange holiday extra service for passengers bound for the Isle of Man speeds along towards the Prairie at Brierfield, No.**44948** is the engine and the date was 6th July 1963. *John E Porter.*

On the Prairie. 1L76, the 7.31am from Blackpool Central to Colne passes the prairie fields at around 9am, heading along to Brierfield. This train was one of the first in our area to use the new B.R. Mark One coaching stock. No.**45442** of Rigby Road depot at Blackpool is the locomotive. In the distance to the right of the railway, is Barden Mill with its new storage shed down by the canal and further right is the winding house of Reedley Colliery. *John E Porter.*

Barden Lane 3.7.61. The beginning of Colne holidays in 1961 proved to be bright and sunny as this view of No.**45156** *Ayrshire Yeomanry* shows. Behind the loco. we see Barden Mill and slightly to the left is the Grenfell works of Messrs. T Haythornthwaite. On days like these the Lancashire countryside was a picture! 1T82 was a period return from Colne to Blackpool Central. *John E Porter.*

Soon we were rolling merrily along towards Burnley, at a spot known locally as the "Prairie". Here the wide open countryside took over once more with playing fields to our left whilst over on the right we were treated to some truly magnificent scenery which stretched from the nearby canal out across the valley and up the hillside towards Pendle Hill. Ahead of us the broad skyline of Burnley could be seen. A vast array of mill chimneys dotted the horizon, the winding house of the nearby Reedley Colliery stood out as did the gasometers of Burnley Gasworks at New Hall Lane. Once across the open spaces of the "Prairie", we reached Barden Lane, it was here that the railmotor halt of Reedley Hallows was to be seen. At Barden Lane two large weaving concerns could be seen, the nearest to the railway being The Barden Mill Co., this tall red brick building looked reasonably modern, its long weaving sheds bordered the railway banking. Some distance away what appeared to be the older of the two mills was owned by Messrs. T. Haythornwaites, it was they, who marketed the branded name of "Grenfell" cloth and this famous name was painted on the slates of the mill roof and is still visible today 40 years later. After Barden Lane speed began to fall on the run into Burnley, we had quickly left behind the bowling greens and gardens that were visible on the left side after Barden Lane where many a retired gent would take a break from playing bowls to watch our seaside special drift past them.

Reedley colliery with its traditional tall winding house, loomed up on our right and soon we crossed the Leeds to Liverpool Canal for the first of many occasions during our run to Blackburn.

Speed Merchant! Rose Grove Driver Ken Garner speeds along towards Burnley, though not at 100mph.........! *John Deluca.*

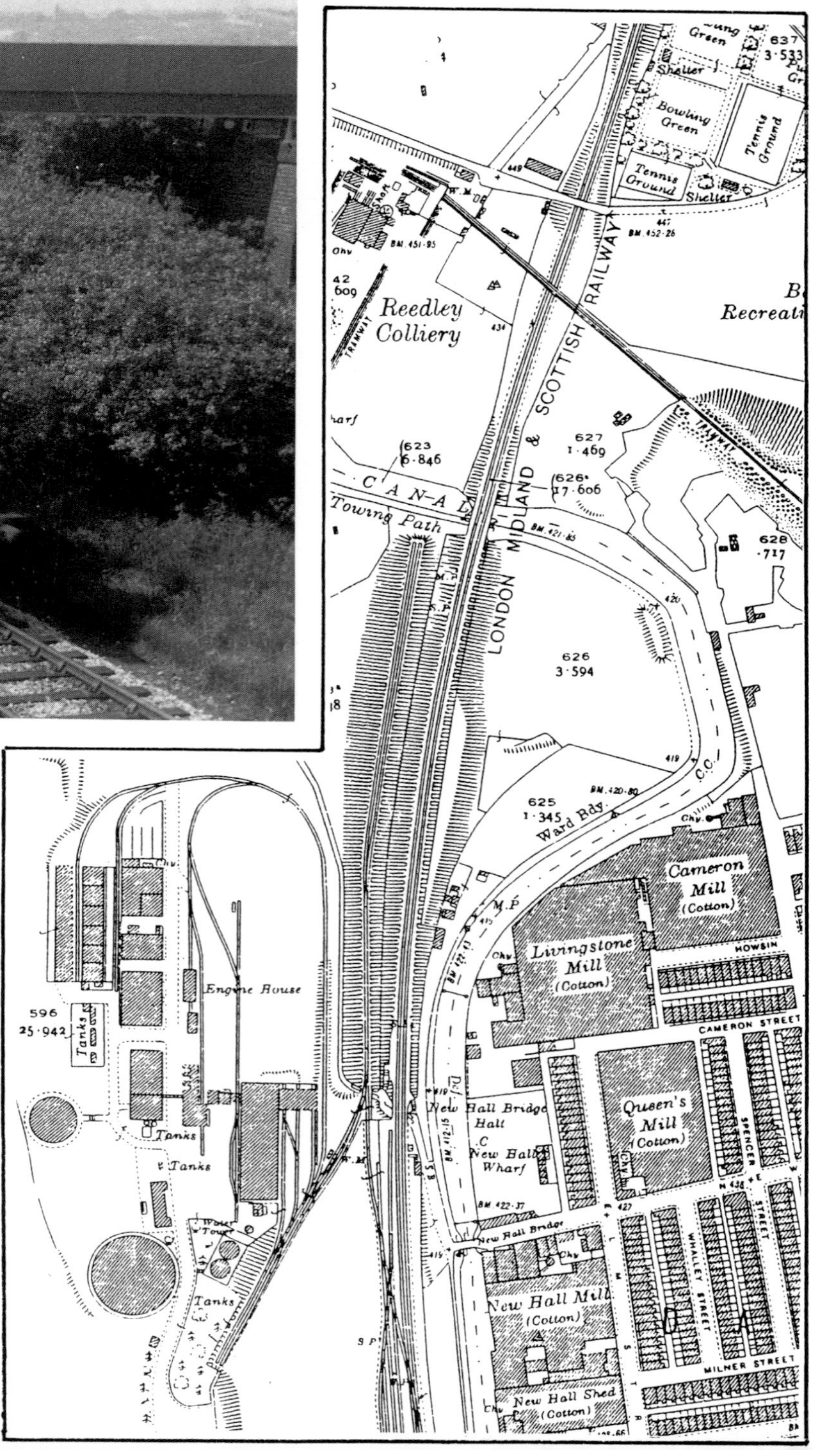

Burnley Corporation Gas Works

Looking West. Beyond Barden Lane a frail looking bridge connected the Reedley Colliery tramway with the storage ground over by the canal. In the early 1950s when the colliery was still in operation the railmotor passes beneath this bridge enroute to Colne. Burnley Corporation Gas Works can be seen in the background. *John E Porter.*

Burnley Gasworks (1). Andrew Barclay loco. works No.1927 and built by coincidence in 1927 became Burnley Corporation Gasworks No.1 together with sister Barclay, Burnley Gasworks No.2, a fireless locomotive of 1938, they must have shunted literally thousands of wagons in and out of the works over the years. *P.A.Lord.*

Burnley Gasworks (2). Class 2 passenger loco No.**40685** drifts swiftly past the gasworks on its run into Burnley. Seen here in its last working week before storage, it had been a regular sight on the local passenger trains between Skipton and Accrington. The gas works are to the left of the picture and over to the far right is the winding house of Reedley Colliery. *John E Porter.*

Burnley Corporation Gas Works

and Danes House Goods Yard.

The long storage sidings for Burnley Gas Works sat high on an embankment made of rubble ash and old bricks. the two sidings stretched all the way from the British Railways connection at Daneshouse goods yard right up to the canal towpath and the sidings ran parallel to the main lines. These two long sidings were constantly full of mineral wagons loaded with coal and the gas works was a hive of activity in the 1950s. Works shunters would be busily trundling loaded wagons over the little concrete bridge that spanned New Hall Lane, taking them into the plant. The massive concrete structure of the plant was an inspiring sight at night when it was illuminated by a large number of sodium lamps which emphasized the escaping steam and gases around the plant.

Whatever time of day you past the works, the smell of coal gas was almost overwhelming, unless of course you liked the smell of rotten eggs !

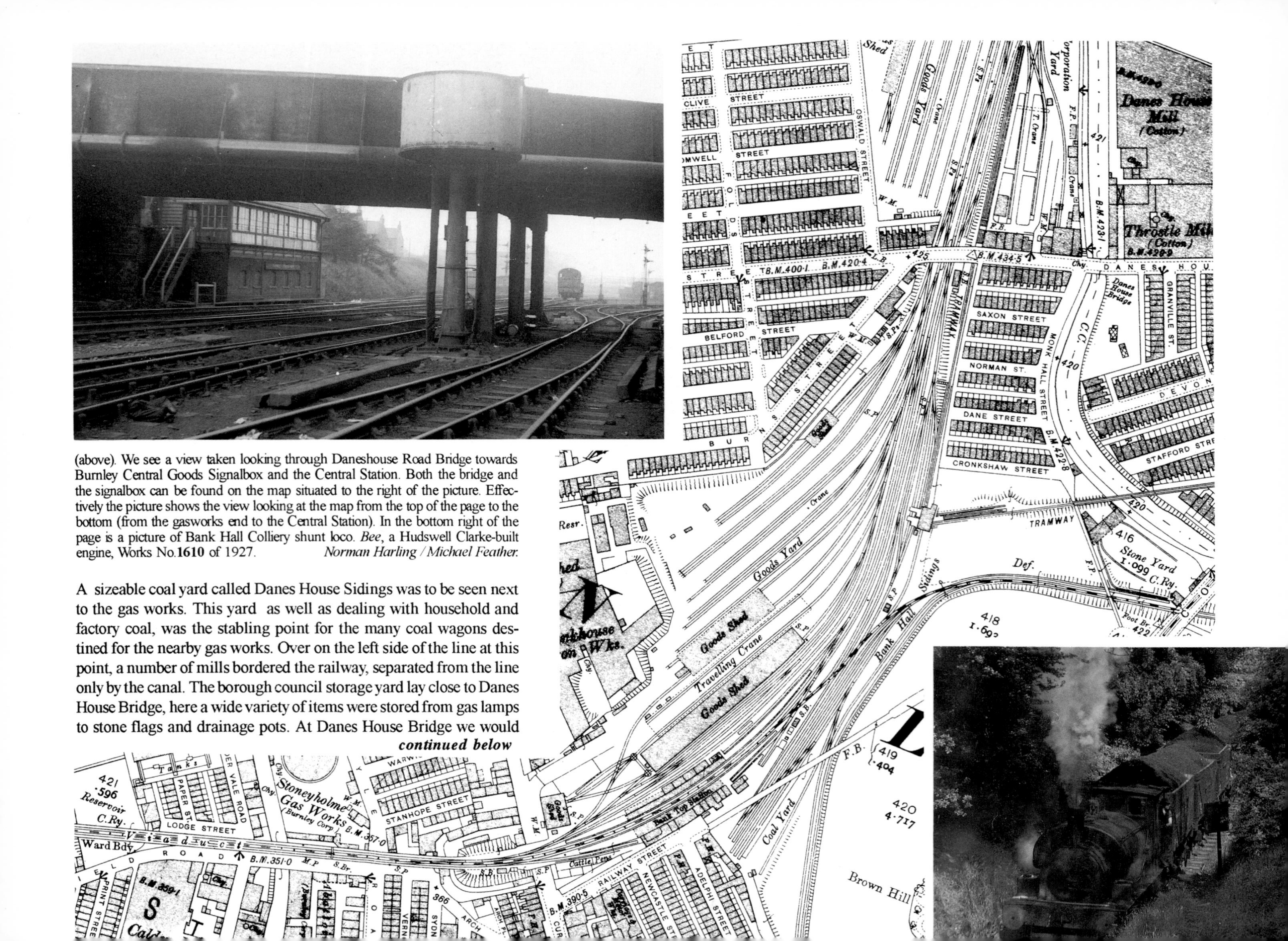

(above). We see a view taken looking through Daneshouse Road Bridge towards Burnley Central Goods Signalbox and the Central Station. Both the bridge and the signalbox can be found on the map situated to the right of the picture. Effectively the picture shows the view looking at the map from the top of the page to the bottom (from the gasworks end to the Central Station). In the bottom right of the page is a picture of Bank Hall Colliery shunt loco. *Bee*, a Hudswell Clarke-built engine, Works No.**1610** of 1927. *Norman Harling / Michael Feather.*

A sizeable coal yard called Danes House Sidings was to be seen next to the gas works. This yard as well as dealing with household and factory coal, was the stabling point for the many coal wagons destined for the nearby gas works. Over on the left side of the line at this point, a number of mills bordered the railway, separated from the line only by the canal. The borough council storage yard lay close to Danes House Bridge, here a wide variety of items were stored from gas lamps to stone flags and drainage pots. At Danes House Bridge we would

continued below

often see two or three engines shunting or taking water from the double sided parachute tank situated next to the bridge. Just beyond the large girder bridge, the main Burnley Central goods yard curved sharply to the right and due to the severe curve, it was not the best of places to shunt. The main line curved away to the left before swinging tightly to the right upon the entering the platforms at Burnley Central. Burnley Central Good Yard signalbox was a large structure set back against the wall near to Danes House Bridge. Between this signalbox and the station were the Bank Hall Colliery exchange sidings, the coal from this pit supplied a number of power stations most notable of which seemed to be the one at Wyre Dock near Fleetwood and in later years the larger 21 ton double door mineral wagons saw regular use on these trains. Visible behind the colliery sidings at Burnley Central was the rear of the Platers and Stampers works, you may recall the tale by Eric Laycock about this firms outing to the seaside in the 1950s, which appeared in *The Railways of Colne*.

Burnley Central Goods Yard and Bank Hall Colliery Exchange Sidings

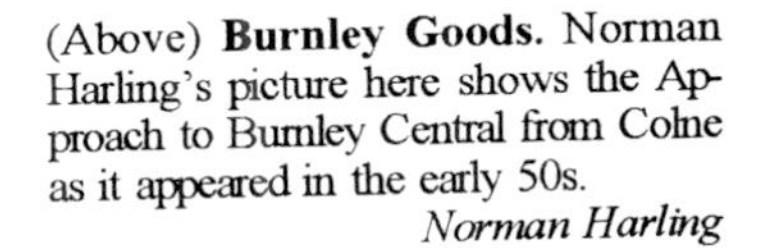

(Above) **Burnley Goods.** Norman Harling's picture here shows the Approach to Burnley Central from Colne as it appeared in the early 50s.
Norman Harling

(Right) **Shunting Staff.** The yard staff at Burnley Central. Driver Wilf Jones and fireman John Deluca are seen here to the left and to their right are Jimmy Riley, Rupert O'Connell Frank Higgins and Lesley Finch. *John Deluca.*

Burnley Pilot. One of the regular shunt drivers at Burnley Central was driver Jimmy Johnson. The 350 H.P.diesel shunts were with us from the dawn of the 60s.One of those often seen at Burnley was 3007 and yes...... you've guessed it, it was nicknamed "licensed to kill"....! *John Deluca*

Busy Burnley (1). With almost a full house the yard at Burnley Central looks to be a thriving freight centre.The new warehouses provided excellent covered unloading facilities.Over on the right the new staff amenity was built around the time the station was modernised in 1964. *Terry Kershaw.*

Busy Burnley (2). Looking the opposite way back towards Daneshouse and Burnley Gasworks.The large travelling crane gantry was one of only four of its type the other three being at Stockport, Rugby and Wolverhampton. The sidings where the Black 5 is seen on the right were the Bank Hall Colliery exchange sidings.
E. Blakey (courtesy of The L and Y Soc.,)

Burnley Central Station. Luke Kaye, at the time a Rose Grove signalman took this atmospheric view of the line looking up the bank towards Burnley Barracks. Just look at all those mill chimneys ! *Luke Kaye.*

Burnley Central station.

We always approached the station at Burnley Central quite slowly, the flanges of the coach wheels binding on the tight curve, the large solid wheels giving off a sort of ringing noise, which at times could be almost deafening. Burnley Central was a really busy station , a very full platform of daytrippers greeted us on lots of occasions, passengers of all shapes and sizes and walks of life squeezed together in readiness to board the holiday excursion. Probably this period in the 1950s would be as about a classless a time as we shall ever see, whilst office workers plainly stood out when seen together with the factory floor staff, whether in their Sunday best or not, all would be thrust together as they jostled for seats on the seaside express.

As we came to a stand at Burnley, all hell let loose.... ! there was one mad dash for seats, we would watch from our vantage point up by the engine as this spectacle took place, it was like watching refugees fleeing a war torn country. You could fairly sense the air of urgency to grab a seat at all costs. Drawing up at Burnley was a must and although the platforms would accommodate ten coach trains, passengers would not walk all the way to the back to find seats, therefore the porters busily slammed doors and waved the driver forward towards the Central station signalbox near to the viaduct. Here we would stand for a few minutes while the remaining crowds boarded the special. This high position on the banking top gave us a fine view of the town at Burnley. By 1960 the new Keirby Hotel, constructed of concrete and brick stood out high above the more traditional stone buildings of the town. Like Smith and Nephews at Brierfield it too had a large neon lit sign on the roof and the lights from the name and the many elevated rooms ensured that the hotel was a very visible landmark at night. In keeping with the gas works area, the Central station had a smell all of its own, this emanated from the knackers yard which was to be found beneath the end of the viaduct. When the Queen paid Burnley a visit by rail in the 1960s, the firm was asked to cease production whilst the Royal visit was taking place. Over the years many complaints were received by the railway from the bone works, in relation to the problem of missiles, that kept crashing down from the viaduct and through the asbestos roof cladding, sending the workers dashing for cover. It seems that over zealous coaling up of engines up at Rose Grove meant that as they travelled light engine tender first to Burnley or Colne, the tender would bounce and lurch upon hitting the point work at the viaduct end and off would fall the odd cob of coal and the asbestos roof down below was no match for a lump of "best Yorkshire hard".

Our departure from Burnley would be slow and noisy, as our engine plodded purposefully up the incline towards Burnley Barracks station. Near to the railway at this point a number of rows of terraced houses could be seen below the railway embankment to our left side. These streets seemed so close together that the bright morning sunlight just didn't appear to penetrate them. Lines of washing straddled the streets and literally dozens of young children played noisily below us apparently oblivious of the fact that the holidays were here. On we would climb past the Bowling Green Hotel, with its little bowling green out at the back. Also next to the railway at this point was the old army barracks building, a gaunt stone structure from a past era.

Burnley Central Station. 1964. These quiet platforms would be transformed at the local holiday fortnight, as hundreds of day-trippers filled the platform area, all eagerly hoping for seats on the many seaside specials which would call en-route to the Lancashire coast. *E. Blakey (courtesy of the L. & Y. Society).*

(below). **Old Faithful.** No.**52179**, seen here behind the station on the goods loop (about 1956,) was the last local "Lanky" locomotive, being withdrawn in August 1960. In the view opposite (top-right), 52179 makes a spirited run out onto the viaduct. In the cab is shunter Jimmy Riley. *Michael Feather.*

All Change. In 1964 work began to rebuild the Central station. the work took the best part of two years to complete.Whilst the subway was being altered a temperary footbridge was in use. On the posters to the left Blackpool's Winter Gardens, advertise that David Whitfield Sheila Buxton and Colin Crompton are doing the summer season shows. *British Railways.*

Up the bank to Rose Grove

Up the Bank. No.**47386** on the Burnley pilot job, pushes No.**52179** up the bank towards Burnley Barracks which can be seen in the far distance framed beneath the signal gantry. Junction mill stands high above Barracks station to the right. In the 1950s there were two Jim Dean's based at Rose Grove. Here we see the older of the two wearing his traditional trade mark flat cap. Note the **L** plate on the front of the pilot engine. In the right hand picture No.**52526** plods steadily up the incline from Burnley as seen from beneath the viaduct in Ashfield Road. Lastly, driver Ellis Nutter gives rear end assistance.

Michael Feather (2) Mick Kelly (1)

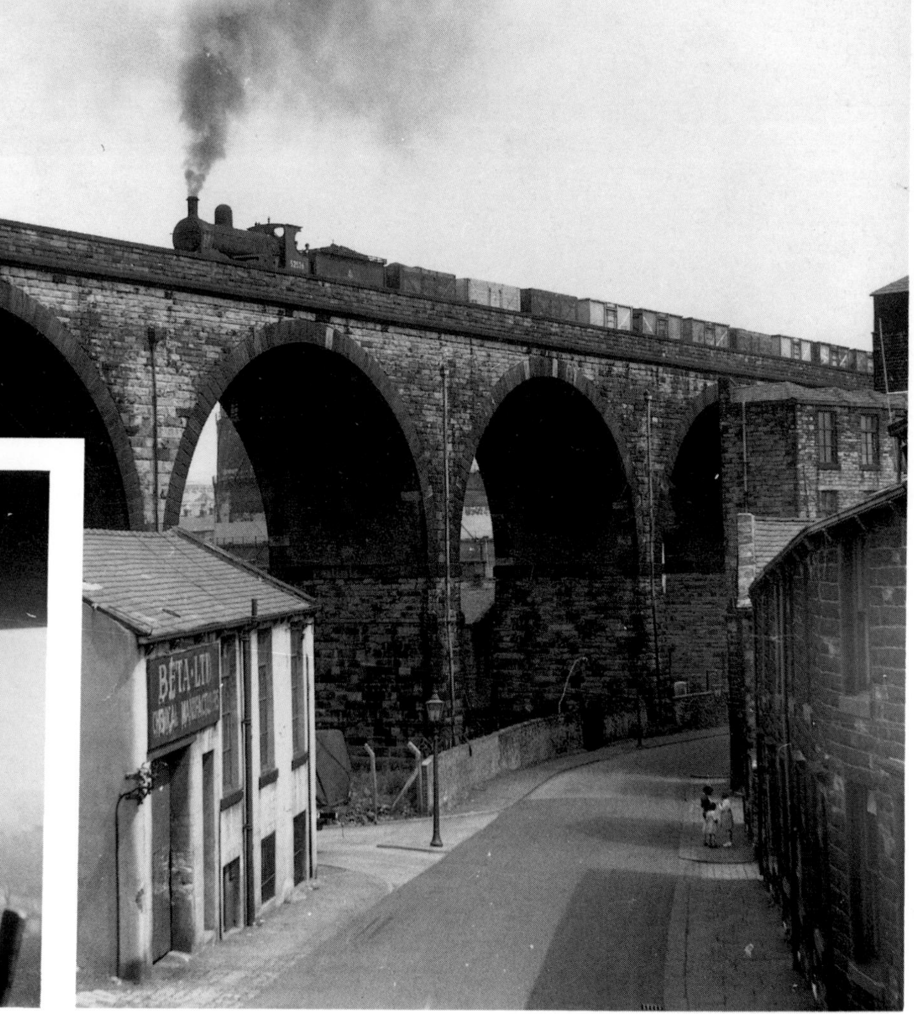

The Dark Satanic Mills in the Song "JERUSALEM" clearly came to mind as we look at the smoggy atmosphere above Burnley. The railway from Daneshouse curved from the left hand distance (beyond the mill chimneys) round through Central Station (hidden behind the coal train and now the line climbs steeply up to Burnley Barracks and Rose Grove beyond. The loco is No.**48124** of Rose Grove shed. *Noel Coates.*

"mill town" Lancashire

Barracks Approach. The climb to Barracks station was always slow and noisy. The engines bark would echo around the town. Ahead of the engine (No.**45388**), is the station at Burnley Barracks, with the station masters house seen close to the canal.
Eddie Bobrowski.

Burnley Barracks station.

Our driver nearly always kept steam on almost to the platform end at the Barracks station such was the drag of the incline at this point, the nine coach load behind the loco. would soon bring us down to walking pace as we drifted through the straight platforms of the station. We had crossed the Leeds to Liverpool canal again at the platform end and as usual over to our right a number of children could be seen climbing on the gas pipe which straddled the canal close by the station. We often commented just how dangerous a play area this particular pipeline was. The waiting crowd upon the platform at Barracks station would look anxiously in the passing compartments of the train, they seemed to be almost peering in at us. By now the train was filling up and the availability of seats let alone empty compartments was somewhat reduced. The still moving train would creep steadily along the platform coming to rest with the locomotive just clear of the main road overbridge which spanned the railway and as the engine passed under the bridge the now lifting safety valves would as a rule send pigeons fluttering off in all directions, beating a hasty retreat from their home beneath the girders of the bridge. Whilst the engine was clear of the darkness of the bridge hole we in our compartment next to the loco. would be sat in semi - darkness. near to the platform end. Under the road bridge a very narrow section of the platform ran along close to the bridge wall. This narrow walkway, was barely wide enough for people to walk in single file, but all too often a mad dash would occur as the daytrippers ran headlong into the darkness of the bridge-hole jostling each other in an effort to find seating up at the front of the train. All too often delays to the train would occur as shoes were lost down between the footboards of the train and the platform edge, in the darkness passengers missed their step as they scrambled aboard and the poor old porters had the job of crawling down to retrieve the lost items of footwear. Looking towards the engine we could see the loco. crew sat out in the sunlight looking back and grinning at the events taking place beneath the bridge. Soon much whistling and waving of arms would indicate that a draw up was needed, with a pop on the whistle the driver would ease his engine forward, small white clouds of steam would drift off the chimney top as the loco. chuffed slowly forward bringing us out of the darkness and into the bright sunlight. A rumble of the brake cylinders beneath the coach told us we were far enough forward to enable the remaining passengers to join the train. Our seaside special had become quite rowdy by now, the wooden compartment walls were quite thin and all the noise and laughter, could easily be heard. You could fairly sense the air of excitement and anticipation throughout the train.

Running into Barracks. The locomotive is just passing over the Leeds to Liverpool Canal upon entering the platform, ahead the overbridges of Junction Street and Padiham Road can be seen spanning the railway. *Noel Coates.*

Mutual Exchange. In the early 1960's the shed staff at Rose Grove went on a number of visits abroad to European depots on a mutual exchange basis to see how the different railway systems worked. These holiday insights into foreign railway working were very popular events. Ready for the off are (standing) Tommy Stubbs, Brian Doe, Bob Broadley, ... ? Brian Perrin and Joe Carroll. (kneeling) John McGee, Harold Leyland, Des Melia and Gordon Langford. They are seen on the Up platform at Burnley Barracks in this mid-sixties picture. *Des. Melia.*

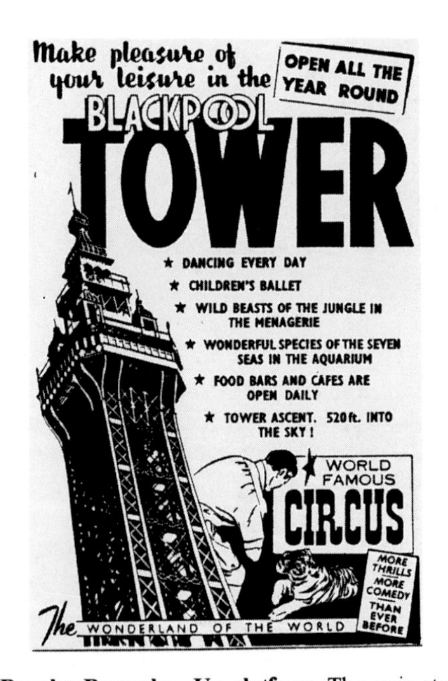

Burnley Barracks - Up platform. The main station building, comprising Booking Office - above at road level - and covered waiting area on the platform below, survived well into the 1970's. Despite the cramped area of the station, a large number of passengers would board the many excursion trains which called during the local holidays. *S. Taylor.*

Burnley Barracks (1). Taken from the Down side platform looking up through the bridges towards Gannow Junction, with the high arched Cavalry Bridge towering above the DMU. The narrow walkway where daytrippers dashed along in the dark can be seen just under the Padiham Road bridge over on the far platform. *S.Taylor.*

BURNLEY BARRACKS

Burnley Barracks (2). Here we see the downside platform with the large Junction Mill in the in the background.The little wooden waiting room was not unlike the one seen at Brierfield. The platform continued down over the canal bridge where the decking was of sleepers. *S.Taylor.*

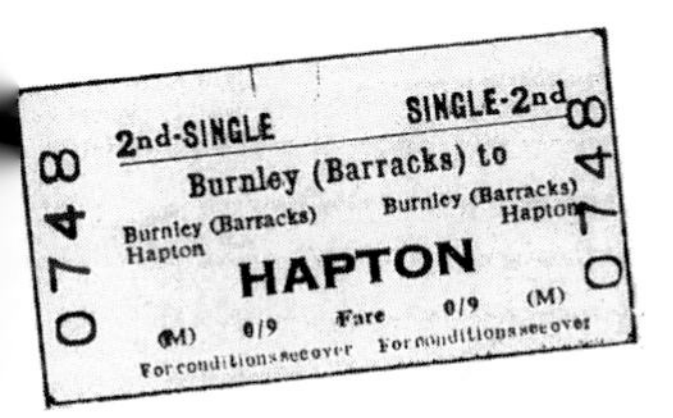

2nd-SINGLE SINGLE-2nd
0748
Burnley (Barracks) to
Burnley (Barracks) Hapton
Burnley (Barracks) Hapton
HAPTON
(M) 0/9 Fare 0/9 (M)
For conditions see over For conditions see over
0748

Holiday Crowd. This is how we remember Barracks station, full of waiting daytrippers anxiously looking out for their seaside special.
Burnley District Library (Lancashire C.Libraries).

Up to Gannow. 1Z31 a Morecambe Promenade excursion, with driver Winston Hartley at the regulator plods up the bank towards Gannow Junction, having called at Burnley Barracks station. Junction Mill towers above the station which is hidden beyond the new overbridge, which was built after Skipton men Billy Walker and John Parish on their "Derby 4" ignited the leaking gas main beneath the bridge causing chaos at Colne holidays in July 1960.
Brian Wrigglesworth.

Looking up to Gannow - as we stood just beyond the overbridge which carried Padiham Road at Burnley Barracks station, this was the view we had looking up in the direction of Gannow Junction. The line was steep at this point, around 1 in 103, and a deep cutting was spanned by the high arched Cavalry Bridge, seen here with a Preston bound dmu passing beneath. As we set off up the bank in our excursion train, the loco's exhaust would be vertical and the noise would reverberate around the cutting sides, the engine clearly "shouting the odds". *S. Taylor.*

Beyond Barracks station a deep cutting opened up, private sidings used to be situated in the open space to our left, an area which was fast becoming a dumping ground for building rubble. As we departed Barracks station and headed up the steep incline towards Gannow Junction and Rose Grove the engines safety valves which had been merrily lifting whilst we had been stood at Burnley Barracks quickly reseated themselves as steam was needed elsewhere, the engines exhaust would now be a vertical column of dark smoke, from the freshly applied coal, which would help maintain steam pressure to Rose Grove. The bark of the engine as it got to grips with the steep grade, echoed around the deep cutting, high above us the arches of Cavalry bridge spanned the railway. On the abutments of Cavalry bridge an elevated walkway ran round the rear of the old army barracks buildings, it was here that children could always be seen running to and fro, they would stop their play briefly to look down at the passing seaside special, waving and shouting to us in a seemingly envious sort of way. The vision of those youngsters up on Cavalry bridge would linger with us for many years as would the memory of the terraced houses further up the incline to Gannow Junction where young mothers would often be spotted hanging out the washing or holding young children in their

Cavalry Bridge. As we slowly plodded up to Gannow, children high above us on the walkway at Cavalry bridge and those playing near the row of houses up above, would wave and shout as we passed by on our way to the seaside. No.**48471** not having stopped at Barracks is doing well up the bank, we in our excursion train would literally plod all the way up the hill. The engines exhaust would be straight up in the sky, the noise deafening and the roar was enough to lift the slates off the house roofs at times.
Noel Coates.

Light Engine to "Grove". The opposite view to the one above, though this time taken from high up the banking near "the Barracks Tavern" pub. Children often waved to us from the houses in the top left of the picture. The new Gannow Jnc. signal box can be seen framed in the arch of the overbridge to the right of the picture. The B.R. "4" was leading L.E. to Rose Grove Shed. *Noel Coates.*

arms, urging them to wave at the passing steam train. We often felt that somehow the world was passing these people by.
At the top of the incline we reached Gannow Junction, it was here that the line from Yorkshire via Copy Pit curved in to join us on our left side. In later years a new British Railways style of signal box would be built in the fork of the Junction, this was in 1964. The old Gannow signal box was positioned on our right at the end of the Down Hump Marshalling Yard. With the climb now over our loco. would be eased back for the short run along past the marshalling yards to Rose Grove station.

Rainy Days. The sun didn't always shine as we left East Lancashire for the coast, but as a rule, by the time Preston was reached, the day was much brighter, the sun was shining and we could fold our rain macs away. No.**44858** on excursion 1T80 climbs away from Cavalry Bridge towards Gannow Junction. Driver Jimmy Cook of Rose Grove and his young fireman Terry Kershaw (below) look down in the dumps as they plod up the incline to Gannow Junction. *Noel Coates*

Gannow Junction

(above) **Gannow Junction.** Coming over the top at Gannow No.**44909** blackens the windows of the houses in Arundel Street and Park Street, the speed limit was 45 mpd here but fat chance of that from a standing start at Barracks station. *Noel Coates.*

Gannow Junction 1957. Two views here showing the old Gannow Junction signalbox in use until 1964.Above is the view looking off the Down hump headshunt towards the Copy Pit route, whilst the picture seen below is from the Up Slow line looking down towards Burnley Barracks.Returning excursions would be nose to tail especially at the illuminations time and most would draw up to the parachute tank here to get water before tackling Copy Pit. *Norman Harling.*

Gannow Junction Signalman. Norman Harling (above), whose excellent pictures are seen here around Gannow Junction, was for many years one of the regular men at Gannow box. So too was Jimmy Whitaker (seen above right, with box lad Peter Dickinson). Peter later became a guard at Rose Grove.In the picture to the right taken on 30th June 1957 No.**72003** *Clan Fraser*, a rare type of loco. to us heads past the Down "Grid" near to Gannow Junction with a Blackpool to York special.

Norman Harling (2) Luke Kaye (1)

Rose Grove Down "Grid"

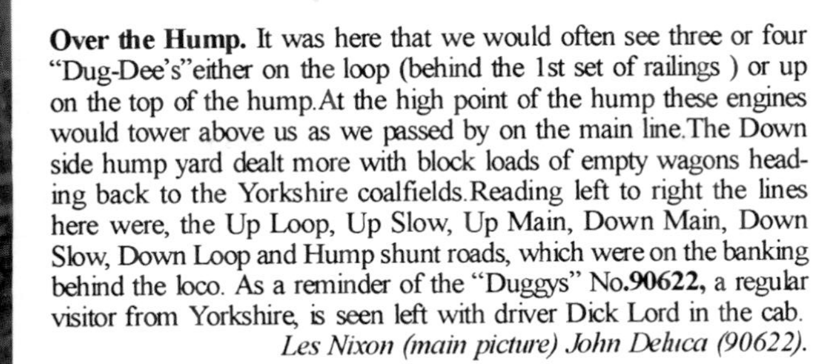

Over the Hump. It was here that we would often see three or four "Dug-Dee's"either on the loop (behind the 1st set of railings) or up on the top of the hump.At the high point of the hump these engines would tower above us as we passed by on the main line.The Down side hump yard dealt more with block loads of empty wagons heading back to the Yorkshire coalfields.Reading left to right the lines here were, the Up Loop, Up Slow, Up Main, Down Main, Down Slow, Down Loop and Hump shunt roads, which were on the banking behind the loco. As a reminder of the "Duggys" No.**90622,** a regular visitor from Yorkshire, is seen left with driver Dick Lord in the cab.

Les Nixon (main picture) John Deluca (90622).

Rose Grove "Yard & East Pilot"

On the "Jocko". On the Down side shunt engine we see left to right, John Eddie Simpson (driver), George Fenton (signalman), Micheal Kerrygewits (shunter), Bill Evans (fireman), Horace Debue (head shunter), Albert Harding, (shunter) and on the running plate Sammy Knox (shunter).
John. Deluca.

LINE SEQUENCE

No 3 P S LOOP
UP LOOP
UP SLOW
UP MAIN LINE
DOWN MAIN LINE
DOWN SLOW
DOWN LOOP
SHUNT LINE

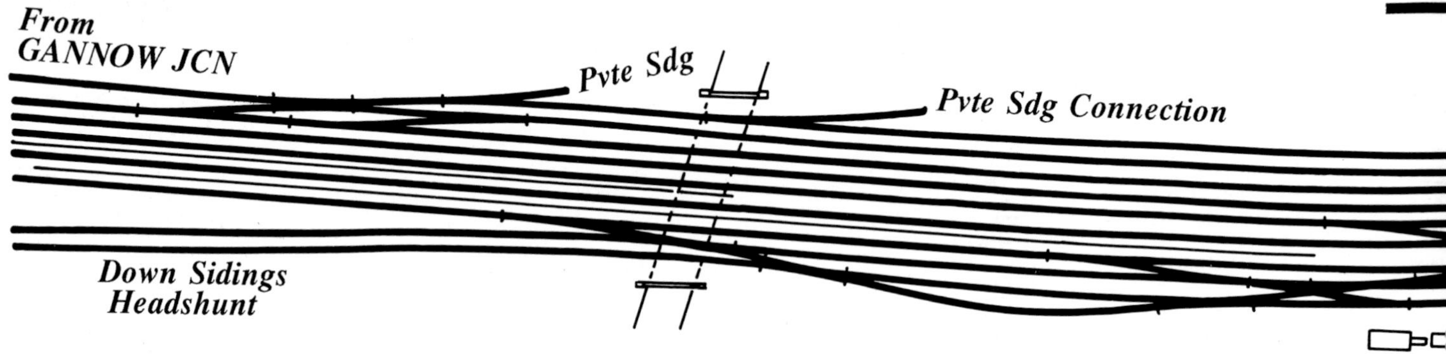

Rose Grove Down Hump Yard.

Over on the Down side hump sidings, or Down "Grid" as it was more commonly called, a greater percentage of the traffic would be formed of empty wagons destined for the Yorkshire coalfields and many trainloads of empty mineral wagons could be seen recessed here.
The large Down Sidings consisted of the local goods warehouse and coal sidings, this warehouse being a substantial red brick structure which stood quite close to the station platform Behind the warehouse were five coal roads which fanned out towards the main marshalling yard. Slightly further over in the Gannow Junction direction was the Down Sidings signalbox, which controlled movements to and from the hump yard. The signalbox was situated at a point where some 20 sidings formed the down yard and in these sidings there was room for around 750 wagon lengths. Whilst many empty wagons were stabled here, many more block trains of empties merely drew up the nearby loop to take water at Gannow Junction, being relieved before setting off up Copy Pit en-route for the Wakefield area. Close to the Gannow Junction end of the Down yard, the Down Slow line was separated from the main line by a blue brick wall lined with heavy iron railings. An even higher blue brick wall supported the Down loop and hump shunt, which sat high above the slow line, this second higher wall also had a heavy railing mounted along much of its length. It was here, high on the Down "Grid", that we would often see two or three "WD's" shunting or taking water all at the same time.

Rose Grove Marshalling Yards.

(a detailed account).

Rose Grove was a very busy freight centre indeed, the two marshalling yards there dealing with literally thousands of wagons every week in the 1950s and early 60s. The greater majority of these wagon loads would be coal traffic, with large amounts coming out of the Yorkshire coalfields. There was however a fair percentage of local coal from such places as Bank Hall colliery at Burnley and this coal seemed destined for the furnaces of powers stations in the region, much of the Bank Hall coal making the journey to Fleetwood for Wyre Dock Power Station. Certain blends of coal were the right grade of fuel for particular types of power station boilers and therefore in the case of Bank Hall colliery, the trains would often depart from Burnley Central and pass by Rose Grove sidings travelling as block loads direct to the power station, with no need for re - marshalling.
In the 1950s household coal and factory coal was still in big demand this coal together with other types of general freight would require shunting at the Rose Grove yards.

Rose Grove East. Looking towards the East box and Gannow Junction, light engine No.**90417** heads for the shed on the bi-lateral Down Slow line The Down Hump yard is to the left whilst the Up yard can just be seen in the far right of this view. *Luke Kaye.*

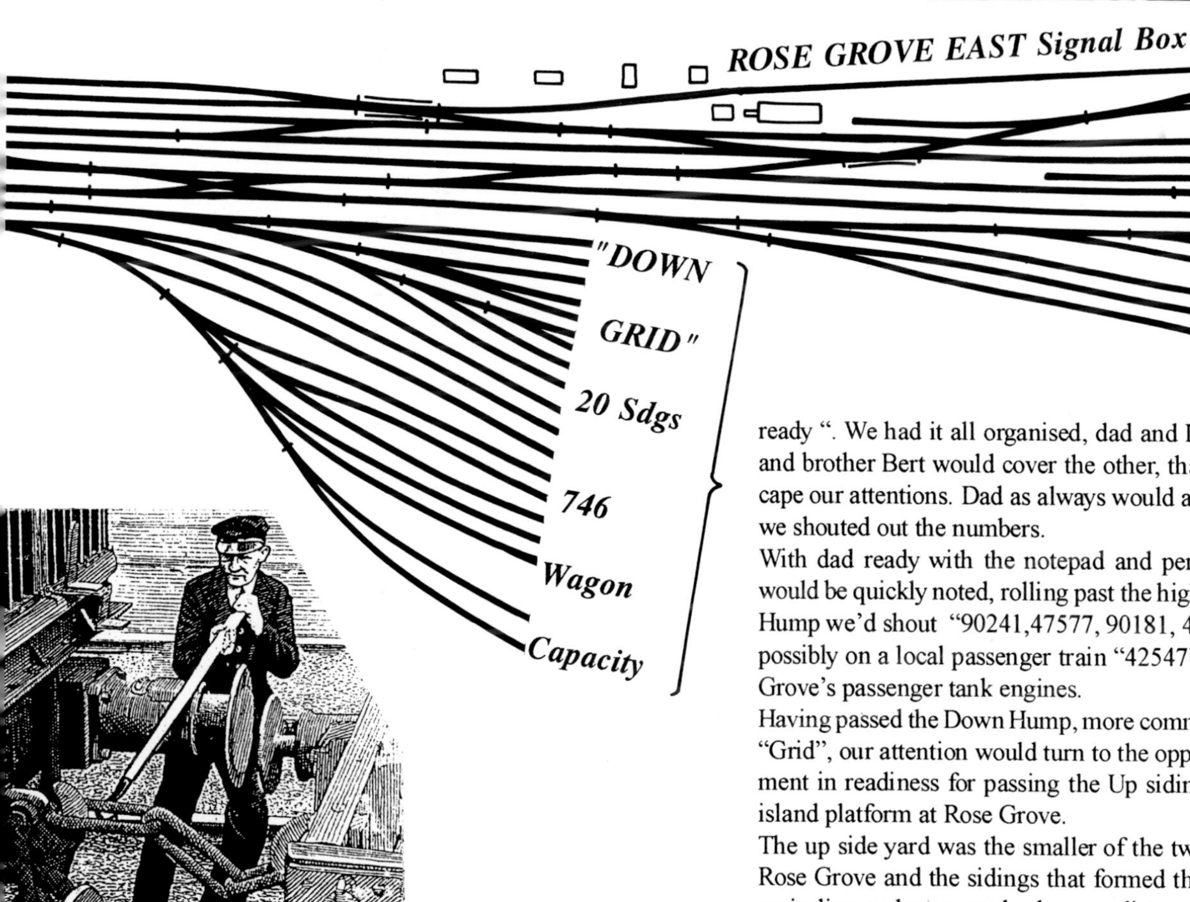

Travelling into Rose Grove.

In order to reach the island platform of the station at Rose Grove, we would pass both the Down and Up sidings at Rose Grove. In view of the engines to be seen , it really was a case of " spotting books at the ready ". We had it all organised, dad and I would man one window and brother Bert would cover the other, that way nothing would escape our attentions. Dad as always would act as numbertaker, whilst we shouted out the numbers.

With dad ready with the notepad and pencil, the engine numbers would be quickly noted, rolling past the high shunt neck of the Down Hump we'd shout "90241,47577, 90181, 42717, 90564 90342" and possibly on a local passenger train "42547", which was one of Rose Grove's passenger tank engines.

Having passed the Down Hump, more commonly known as the Down "Grid", our attention would turn to the opposite side of the compartment in readiness for passing the Up sidings as we approached the island platform at Rose Grove.

The up side yard was the smaller of the two hump yards situated at Rose Grove and the sidings that formed the yard sat lower than the main line and were set back some distance from the station. There was a goods loop and three reception sidings before the actual sidings began to fan out. As a rule the first of the dead-end roads was always full of brake-vans, these would tend to be a variety of ex L.M.S. types together with a number of the later B.R. standard brake-vans which were based on the L.N.E.R design.

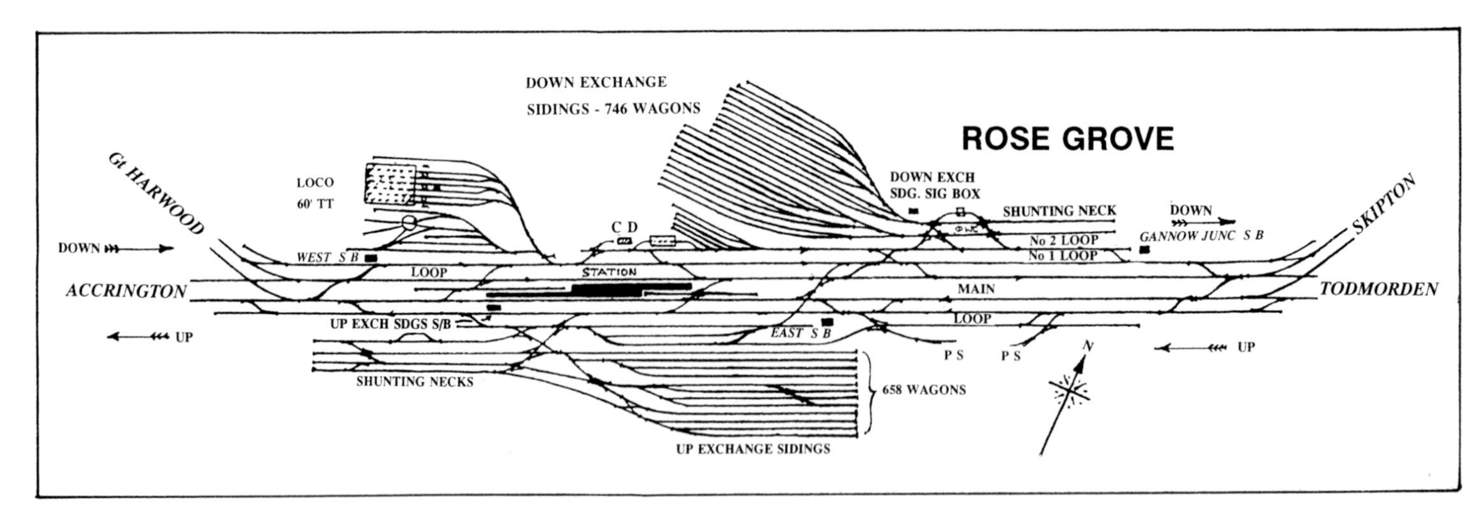

(page right) **Rose Grove Up Hump Yard.** Although both yards are visible in this picture, the Up yard is the main one in this view. Judging by the number of wagons in the foreground things are certainly busy, shunting a thousand wagons a shift was not uncommon in the 1950s.The 8F in the background is approaching the station (which was just out of the picture to the left) with one of the many Burnley-Wyre Dock coal workings in the 1960s. *Bill Hurst.*

"Down the slot". Often termed going "down the slot", being put down the slow lines was a common occurrence on freights, Rose Grove's slow lines were capable of handling passenger trains. I have even seen corridor stock with passengers go over the Up Side Hump at Rose Grove !.... No.**90728** is overtaken by Low Moor Black 5 No.**44694** speeding past on the Main line with a Bradford -Blackpool working in the early 1960s. *Eric Laycock.*

As we passed Rose Grove East signalbox, the tension would mount again and as we began to roll through the platform, the engine numbers would again come thick and fast. Upon coming to a stand at the platform end one day we saw Nos.52179, 47333, 90183, 44948,42716, 42900.

Just across from us, over on the Down main line and by the loop, was the high blue brick wall where locomotives came on and off the shed and between this point and the shed roads we would see a host of motive power, both Bert and myself would be busily shouting out numbers whilst dad quickly jotted them down using his little pencil and pad. With a sense of urgency in our voices we'd shout "47386, 42898, 44940, 52458, 90420, 46147,45216, 90291, 44492, 42545". The engine shed was always full of life and movement and the air around by Rose Grove was generally smoky at the best of times and the smell of burning coal and warm oil lingered everywhere. Many of the locomotives "logged" in dad's notepad would be seen daily as we journeyed to and fro on our week of day trips on the "Runabouts". Some of the engines seen on the shed would be so grimy that the number on the cabside was simply not visible, then maybe later in the same week someone may have rubbed the number with a oily rag, which would then give us one more positive sighting to add to the collection.

Rose Grove Up Hump Yard.

On the Up side at Rose Grove (towards Preston), there was a loop and three reception lines together with 12 storage sidings capable of holding more than 650 wagon lengths. Goods trains would arrive along the reception roads from the East end (Gannow Junction) and come to rest opposite the station platform, where the train engine would hook off and run light engine to the nearby loco. shed. The shunters would turn out and lengthen the couplings and mark the cuts on the wagons in readiness for the shunting to start. As time went on most of the wagons became fitted with "Instanter" couplings, which could be mounted in either the long or short position. In the short position the couplings kept the buffers of the wagons fairly well tight together, but if the couplings were dropped into the long position then a lot of play resulted between the wagons. This made shunting a lot easier and it was possible to unhook the various wagons with the train on the move by simply getting the driver to ease off or push onto the wagons at certain points. There was a hook on the middle link of the "Instanter" coupling and the shunters would slip the curled end of their shunt pole into the hook and with a flick of the wrist, the coupling would drop into the long position. Sometimes they would encounter a heavy screw coupling and as a rule there would be much muttering under the breath as they had to crawl underneath to slacken the screw thread off by hand. The common term for couplings was "Shackle" and shunting the wagons out was known as "Raffling them". The little shunt engine would back onto the prepared train and make ready to draw sections of the heavy load up the incline of the hump, which ran beneath the main road bridge that was Liverpool Road. The shunt engines in the 1950s were usually the ex L.M.S. class 3F tanks such as No.**47577** and they were often nicknamed "Jocko's", this being a general term for shunt engines as a whole. Getting these heavy portions of the train up the hump or "Grid" was no easy task and often there would be some real exhibitions of fireworks as the little "Jocko"struggled to grip on the climb towards the headshunt. When the portion of train finally made it up the incline, a series of whistles could be heard, which indicated to the various staff which sidings the wagons were to be "knocked into". Whistles were used as a method of signalling at Rose Grove because of the inability of the shunters to see each other. The men who actually threw over the points in the sidings were referred to as "Knobbers-Up" and the men who rode the wagons into the sidings and braked them were called "Runners". This latter job was probably the most dangerous on the railway and the number of injuries over the years must have been endless, broken limbs etc., not to mention the occasional fatality. Shunting was however an art and watching it could be fascinating, some shunters making it look so easy.

Once trains had been prepared in the sidings, they would await the arrival of the train engine, more often than not one of Rose Grove's "Austerity" 2-8-0s or something similar. Then it would be a case of let battle commence, as the heavy train struggled to climb over the hump. Fireworks were often the order of the day before the lengthy train began to roll down the West side of the hump. How I wish that I had £1 for every time I've watched a "Dug Dee" stagger over the top of the Up " Grid" at Rose Grove.

Double - Headed "Duggies"

"Attacking the Hump",11.5.63. Nos.**90204** and **90632** give a show of strength as they take a run at the Up Hump at Rose Grove. From the sidings to the Liverpool Road overbridge there was little room to get hold of the train in order to hoist it over the top comfortably and as a result fireworks ensued. The old "dug - dee" would waddle from side to side struggling for grip. With the super power of two Austerities, the job was a piece of cake. *Geoff Robinson.*

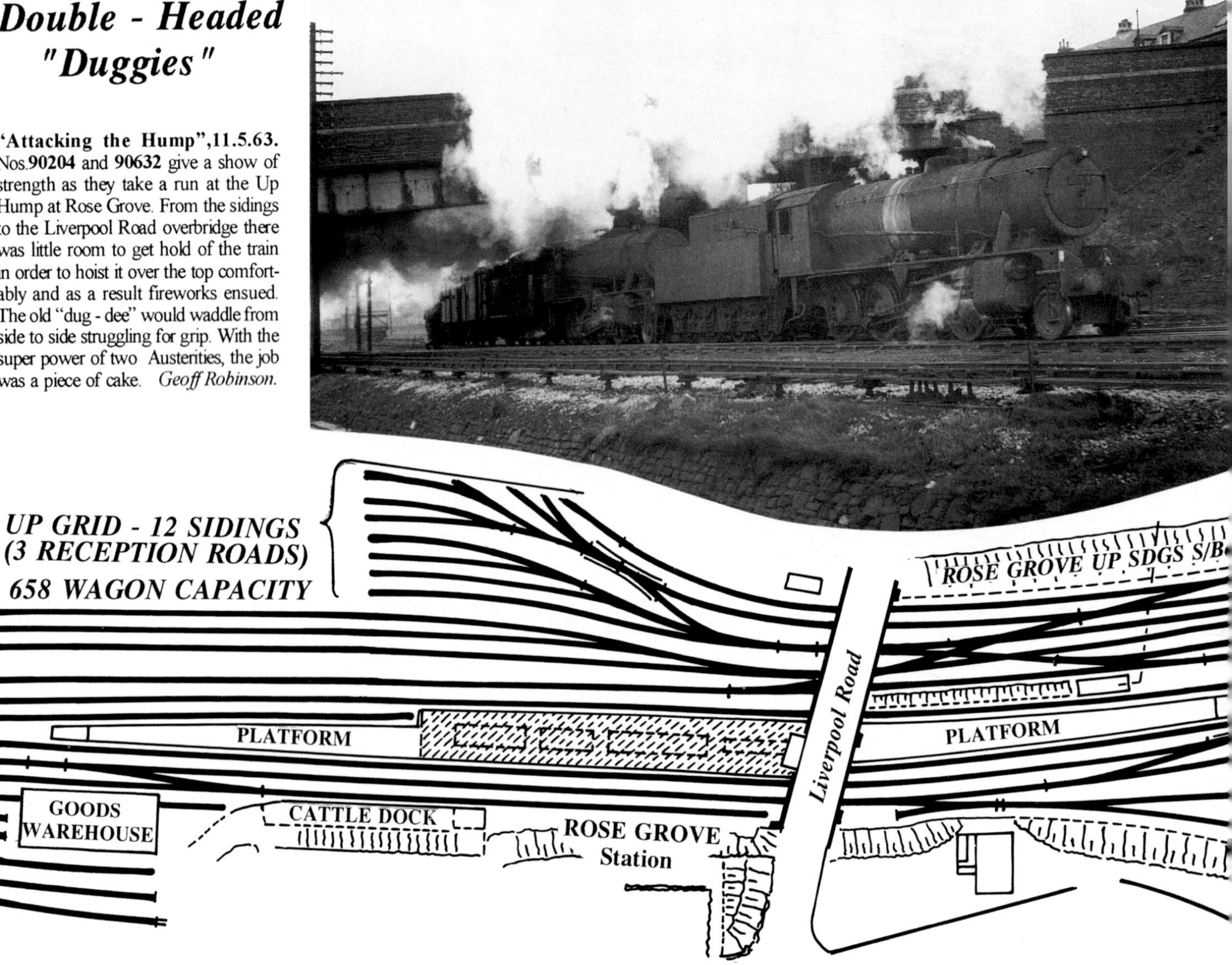

ROSE GROVE

In the Bay. The "Puffing Billy" takes a rest in the bay at the east end of Rose Grove,having worked through to Blackburn with passengers. It was then booked to travel empty via the Padiham loop line to the bay platform at Rose Grove. Here the crew would grab a quick break at 10am before working the 10.14am to Colne. The crew would use the porters room at the platform end as a messroom. Seen in the cab is Arthur Green (passed man) His mate on the platform, we can't place but the chap on the right is porter Dick Westwell who lived at Hapton and whose brother was a driver at the shed. *Michael Feather.*

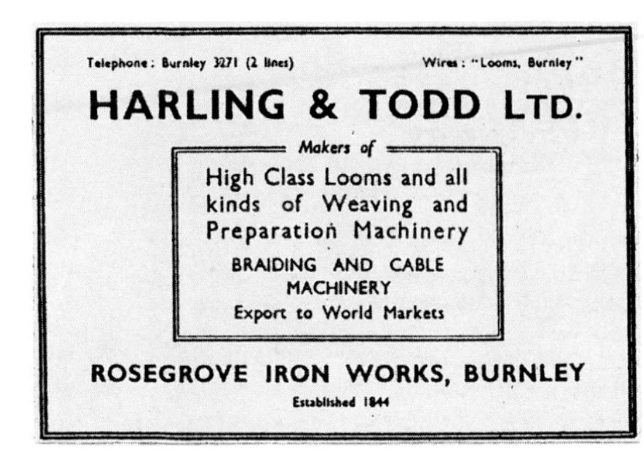

Up Side Shunt. Fireman Terry Kershaw is busily pushing wagons up the headshunt on the Up " Grid " . Behind the loco which is No.**48348**, we see the Up Sidings signalbox and beyond the platform is the shed entrance with the famous blue brick wall. The shed lies out of sight to the left. *Terry Kershaw.*

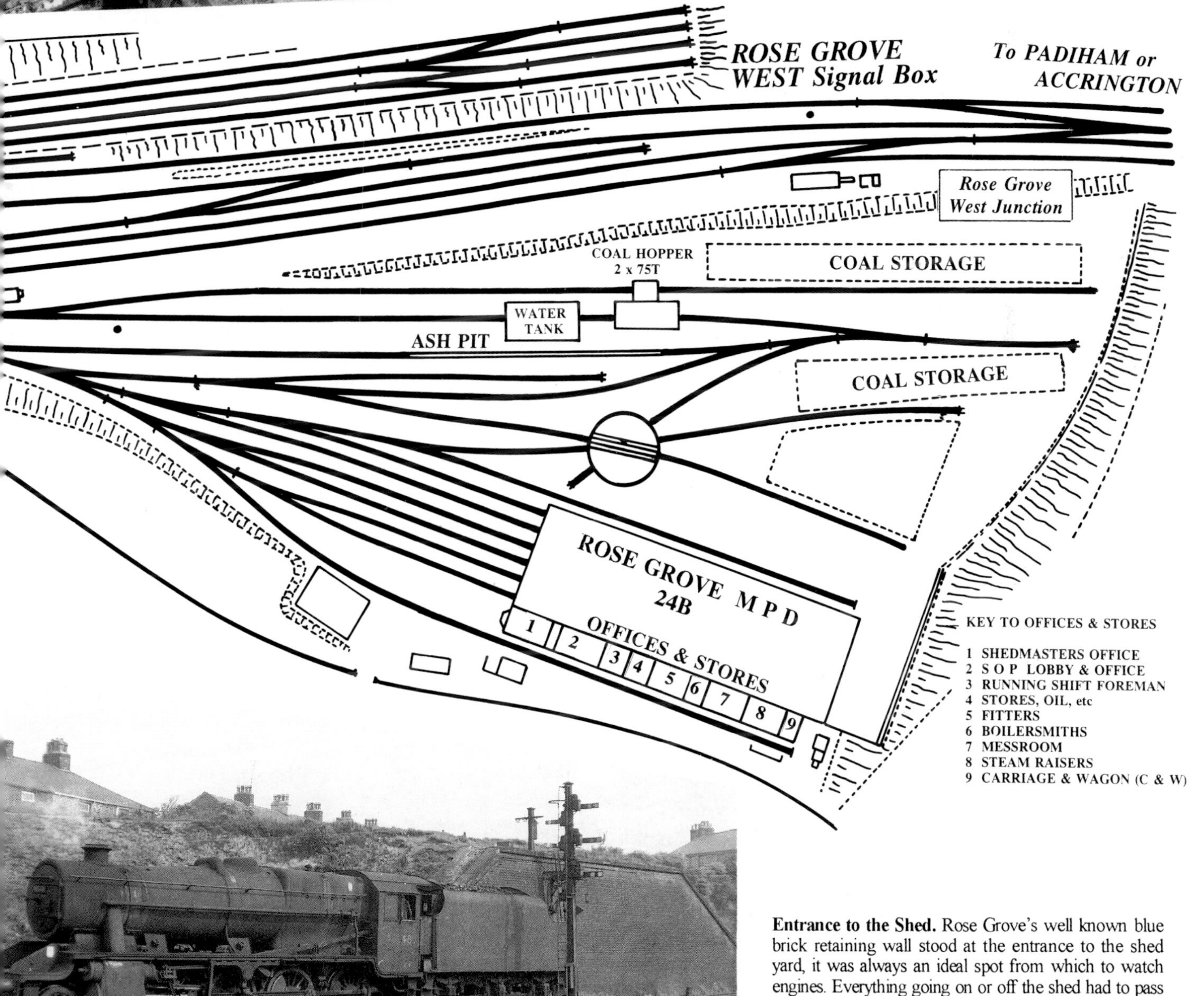

Entrance to the Shed. Rose Grove's well known blue brick retaining wall stood at the entrance to the shed yard, it was always an ideal spot from which to watch engines. Everything going on or off the shed had to pass this point. *Ken Stout.*

Notes on staffing of the Rose Grove marshalling yards.

In the late 1950s Eric Laycock transferred from the carriage shunt at Colne to become a station foreman on the platform at Rose Grove and very smart he looked in his fine new uniform. The job at Rose Grove was right up Eric's street, the Rose Grove station office staff, foreman ,inspectors etc. handled a very busy part of the local rail network. The operation of the marshalling yards came under their control as did all the guards based at Rose Grove. When Eric moved to the station there, the office compliment included three chief inspectors who were Jack Gerrard, George Stansfield and Tommy Gillet. Three yard inspectors on the Down side and three on the Up together with three yard foremen. The number of guards was 72 although there had been 84 guards at one time. On the platform at Rose Grove the offices were as follows. As you came down the staircase from Liverpool Road, the booking office faced you, then it was the Station Masters Office and next came the Admin. Office, where Eric did the paper work as well as doing his platform duties etc. The little telegraph room came next followed by the waiting rooms. Towards the Burnley end of the island platform the Chief Inspectors office and the guards room could be found and right on at the end was the little staff messroom used by the platform staff and visiting traincrew, who having left their train in the bay, adjourned to this room for their "snap". Eric's duties included seeing the trains away and assisting his immediate boss in the control of operations in and around the station and yards. George Stansfield, the inspector over Eric would often swap places with him in order that Eric could learn to handle all manner of problems that may arise, this grounding in the job proved invaluable in coping with events over the years.

The big boss over all, the Yard Master at the time was one G.W.C. Smith, nicknamed General Water Closet Smith ......! He was in total control over the yards, the station etc. and at the time it was a very important position. Rose Grove didn't answer to Manchester or some other divisional base. Instead, each morning the boss would arrive prompt at nine o'clock and, taking off his large homburg hat, Mr. Smith would place a call through to Euston to the head office to make his report of the freight situation at the marshalling yards that particular morning. Such was the volume of coal traffic from the Yorkshire coalfields at this period in the 1950s, that on occasions the yards were full at Rose Grove, as were the reception sidings, and the coal trains would be kept going past the marshalling yards onto Accrington and there they would head off up Baxenden bank, travel over to Bury and on to Todmorden, after which they would make their second climb of Copy Pit before arriving again at Rose Grove, many hours later. It sounds ludicrous, but that's the way it was in those very busy days.

To get back to General Water Closet Smith, one day as he made his daily call to Euston, he stood waiting for the switch boards along the line to connect him, (incidentally he always stood to attention as if he was speaking to the Queen). With the big old black telephone receiver gripped firmly in one hand he heard a faint mutter down the line and in a mad panic began to shout "HELLO, HELLO, HELLO, can you hear me ...., what do I sound like to you"! and from a crossed line on the telephone a voice answered back "Like a pratt"....!

Like Mr. Smith, little Jacky Gerrard (seen in the photo. at his retirement presentation) was a very conscientious boss, for when coming to work on the afternoon shift at 2 pm., he would set off and wander round the sidings, checking up on wagons etc. and when he eventually sat down in the office it could be all of 2 hours later and then he would hold an inquest as to why certain wagons still hadn't moved from the day before. He would then issue orders like "Get them sorted"

In the same retirement group picture you may note Tommy Gillet, another of the station inspectors. Apparently, when the new diesel railcars came on the scene, a special staff outing took Rose Grove staff to Morecambe for the day and whilst at the funfair Tommy was seen to be riding on his own on the carousel. He was sitting on one of the big horses going up and down. Next day back at work, word of Tommy's ride had reached the ears of the yard staff, many of whom were born mickey takers. During that day wherever Tommy past the men, they wouldn't say a word but they would pretend they were riding a carousel horse and begin to bob up and down, mimicking the horse ride. By the end of the day Tommy was red faced and livid with rage.

Van load of rum.

Occasionally, Eric became involved with incidents related to the marshalling yards, the van load of rum was one such incident.

One night amidst the hectic shunting that was taking place, a wagon got away on one of the shunters and with a sickening thud it rammed another vehicle. As the worried shunter surveyed the damage he noticed that a barrel was leaking in the van. This turned out to be full of rum, which was now leaking onto the floor....! "Quick" he shouted as he dashed into the shunters cabin "Get- thee-sen a pot or summat" and he quickly explained about he leaking spirits. All hell let loose...! There was a mad scramble to find anything that would hold the demon drink. Pans, washed out bean tins, pop bottles, you name it, they used it. You never saw such frantic activity.

The following day when Eric was on late turn, the boss called him into the office. The boss at that time Freddie Port, said "Now then Eric I'd like you to take these two gentlemen down the sidings to where that rough shunt was done last night, and show them the wagon etc."

It turned out that the men were from the Customs and Excise department and upon arriving at the scene of the incident, one man took out a trowel and proceeded to remove part of the top ash and began placing it into a bag. When Eric enquired just what he was doing the chap said that when analysed, the ash would reveal the rum content and they would therefore be able to account for the amount of spillage. Eric burst into laughter, "You having me on" he said. The man commented "Not in the slightest". With the ash safely in the bag Eric escorted the two men along to the shunters cabin where an inquest was held as to what happened. "Right" said the Customs man "You lot were all present last night, when this incident occurred". As he spoke he opened his brief case and handed each man a statement which read to the effect that none of them had removed or consumed any of the rum in question. Leaving the men to sign their statements the Customs men nipped along to see the yard inspector Jimmy Foster at the station and he was issued with a statement as well. When the Customs men had departed, Jimmy confided in Eric, saying "I can't sign this, they've all had some of that rum". Back in the shunters cabin, the head shunter, was a big lad called Perkins, "built like a house-side" and fresh out of army service, he became aware of Jimmy Foster's intentions regarding the statement. Apparently he stormed

Presentation. Little Jacky Gerrards retirement in the late 1950s prompted this gathering on the platform at Grove. In the picture we have from left to right, Fred Foster (Up Side inspector), Jacky and Mrs.Gerrard (Jacky was a chief inspector), behind them is Tommy Gillet, (often referred to as Tommy Gillette, Like the razors). He was a chief inspector. Doing the presenting is yardmaster Freddy Port and behind Freddy is Eric Laycock, (station foreman), and on the far right is James Hemingway, (opposite shift foreman). Note the B.T.C. uniforms. *Eric Laycock.*

into Jimmy's office and grabbed hold of him by the lapels and slid him up the wall, shouting "SIGN IT....... OR YOUR WIFE'S A B****:Y WIDOW...."!

Jack Harrison the Yardmaster.

Eric joined Jack one day down at Rose Grove West Junction to measure up an accident scene, upon their return to the station John Willy Dyson who was the Up "Grid" inspector shouted over to them "Er .... Mr. Harrison could I have a word"?

Over on the up sidings a conference was taking place, all the chief inspectors were present including Tommy Gillet and all the shunting staff. "Now then" said Mr. Harrison "What's the problem". John Willy Dyson then went on to explain that the yard staff were refusing to turn out to shunt, because he had sent the bottom man, (that's the chap who follows the wagons into the sidings and brakes them) to cover the "Knocker-up" as well. In effect they were a man short and John had asked the men to help out by having one person do both jobs, but they had refused and downed tools. "Right, let's discuss this sensibly" said Mr. Harrison. "There are two methods of shunting in use here from what I've seen, on the one hand we knock wagons down into the yard with somebody catching them or we follow each move in and out of the sidings, which is what we are asking of you today. On the other hand there's another method which seems to operate when Burnley football club are playing at home.......!, NOW GET YOUR BACKSIDES OUT THERE AND GET ON WITH IT........"!

The stunned workforce, realising that Jack Harrison had called their bluff went about their shunting. What they hadn't realised was that Jack had been down at Turf Moor watching Burnley play on a number of occasions and he had seen some of the staff from the marshalling yards who should have been at work playing "hooky", whilst their mates covered for them.

Down at the shed...things that go missing!

Now and again Eric Laycock would have cause to visit the engine sheds for one reason or another. Uniform clothing and overalls were all kept at the shed and Eric nipped along to the stores to get some overalls for one of the lampmen. In the stores Eric talked to Tommy Bridge. "Right, go and get yer-sel some" said Tommy. "No yer won't" bellowed the stores boss, "Don't let him in there, he'll nick summat..."! and with that the ratty stores boss edged round the front of his desk and went in the back to get the overalls himself. Quickly thinking, Eric spotted a row of brand new twill "Pea" jackets hung on hooks along the wall side. He grabbed one and put it on, hastily fastening up the buttons, just as the storeman returned with the pair of overalls. The storeman seemed oblivious to the fact that Eric was now sporting a new coat and he handed over the overalls without pausing for a second glance. It was some time later before Eric told the storeman about the jacket and he commented to him "I only took it because you made me out to be a thief"

Jack Harrison had always said that he would love a roll top desk and even though he was the yardmaster, he hadn't got one. One Saturday morning Eric walked up the line from the station at Rose Grove to the shed in a real pea souper of a fog. It was a day when you could barely see your hand in front of you. As he reached the shed he saw that the main offices were being repainted and standing outside in the open was a very nice roll top desk. The painters took it and placed it in the buildings by the main entrance. Enlisting the help of Dick Westwell and Walter Windle as well as Archie Harker, they retrieved the roll top desk and slid it along the rail top down to the shed outlet, which was near to the station. The railtop was damp and wet and the base of the desk slid easily along the wet rail. They continued to slide the desk up to the goods warehouse near to the station's island platform all under the cover of the thick fog. They had arranged with the local van driver Johnny Pollard to put the desk into a railway van, so that he could nip down to Jack Harrison's house with it. Shortly afterwards extensive enquiries were made regarding the missing desk, but the facts of just how it was spirited away never came to light, and in the eyes of the elated Jack Harrison, young Eric Laycock could do no wrong!

RULE 117—CODE OF AUDIBLE SIGNALS FOR HUMP SHUNTING

Except where special instructions are issued to the contrary, where klaxon horns, gongs or bells are provided in connection with hump shunting, the following codes for signalling to Drivers will apply:—

Signal	Indicates
One	Hump slowly.
Two	Hump fast.
Three	Stop.
Four	Draw back from hump.

Rose Grove West end. This truly classic view by Bill Hurst shows a wealth of detail. In the foreground "No.**8448**" stands on the Up Hump, the driver is taking "a fiver" and having a read of his newspaper. The Up Sidings signalbox is to the right and the loco. depot is across on the Down side. Over to the left of the picture we see the old red brick "Lanky coal hole" and the more modern coaling plant. The smaller picture to the left here is of No.**42926** shunting the yard, Bill Isbinski (shunter) leans over the tender, Roy Disley (fireman), looks through the cab window and over in the corner the driver is Jimmy Johnson. *John Deluca.*

On the Up "Grid"

Up"Grid" shunt. Drawing into the Up platform in our excursion train. This is the view we would often have of the Up Hump with the pilots shunting the yard. Nos.**47575** and **52216** are seen tugging hard at a long string of old wooden wagons. Shunting like this required patience and experience and generally was a work of art. In the smaller picture here to the left , No.**45580** *Burma* drops down the other side of the hump, ready to run up towards Hapton. A good guard was needed on these trains to prevent breaking loose as the train gathered up and then eased out again.

Michael Feather / Geoff Robinson.

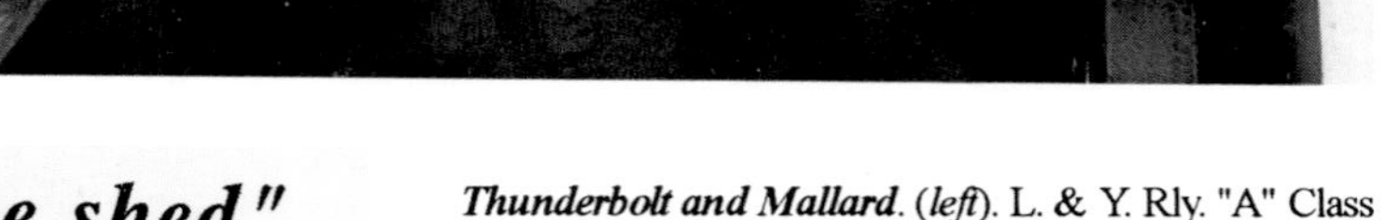

"On the shed"

Thunderbolt and Mallard. (*left*). L. & Y. Rly. "A" Class No.**52369**, the regular engine on the 3.15 Padiham trip job was known to local spotters as *Thunderbolt and Mallard* in the early 1950s. The name was written in chalk on the engine splasher and was still visible when the engine was withdrawn in 1956. The loco is seen here on the shed at Rose Grove on 25th August 1955. (*left upper*). Two more old soldiers from "Lanky" days were Nos.**50651** and **50652**. Whilst in good order they would never really work again after the local push-pull services ended in 1956. Soon they would be wiped off the books and sent for scrap. (*above right*). The travelling M.I.C. coach would do the rounds of all the sheds, giving the lads training and refreshers on the various types of fittings and valves to be found on the engines,. The types of steam brakes, injectors, etc. all varied from engine to engine. The different types of motion and valve gar were also on display. In this view we see drivers Des Melia and Hughie Wearden (2nd and 3rd from the left) together with other "Grove" men, receiving instruction from Inspector Jack Cudworth. On the page below we see (*left*) No.**45705** *Seahorse* of Blackpool resting on the shed prior to running L.E. to Accrington to work the 1/45pm S.O. to Blackpool Central on 11th May 1963. (*right*). Driver Dick Lord oils round his loco. on the shed (we saw Dick earlier on No.90622 on the Down "Grid". (*Lower left*). ... no, the "W.D's" weren't such bad riders that the men needed taking home in wheelbarrows. It was just Des Melia and a mate larking about as passed cleaners. (lower right). Finally, leaving Rose Grove in our non-corridor compartment this is the view we always had upon passing the shed. *Pictures by Brian E. Morrison, F.W. Shuttleworth, Des Melia, Geoff Robinson, Barry Atkinson, Bill Hurst and S. Taylor.*

'SEAHORSE' AT ROSE GROVE.
45705

Rose Grove Motive Power Depot (24 B)

(a brief guide to the facilities).

The motive power depot at Rose Grove was situated on the down side of the line. Access to the shed was via the down goods line and the entrance to the shed yard was adjacent to a high blue brick retaining wall, this wall in turn was quite close to the main road bridge which crossed all the lines at right angles at this point, (Liverpool Road). The layout of the shed yard was quite spacious, the servicing facilities were situated to the left whilst the shed roads and shed itself were over to the right, also on this right side a large banking could be seen, made out of a mountain of ash and debris. The colour of this banking ranged from black to light grey and white, grass just never seemed to grow on this sulphurous ridge. The banking was a favourite place with trainspotters, from this elevated position they could see whatever moved around the shed also what was passing on the main lines nearby. The whole of the shed yard and shed itself appeared to be built on a mountain of old ashes. The shed had six roads and covered accommodation was available for around 24 engines, additional storage being found on both sides of the shed building where especially in later years rows of redundant engines would be stored. The shed was modernised to varying degrees over the years, the shed building itself being extended and re-roofed and the old "Lanky coal hole" replaced by a modern concrete coal hopper with two bunkers each holding 75 tons of coal. A mechanical ash plant was provided and in 1946 the turntable was removed and replaced by a larger 60 foot table which was placed nearer to the shed, causing a slight remodelling of the shed layout. At the shed approaches a hard standing area made of concrete had been provided as well as a number of red bricked buildings, these new structures were designed for use with the oil firing proposals which never came.

In the 1950s large stock piles of coal were to be seen down the side of the shed and a wide variety of railway staff would turn up on a Sunday to off load coal from wagons onto the stockpiles. Each man had to empty a wagon to qualify for the Sunday rate and the volunteers ranged from shed staff to porters from the nearby stations and even the station master at Hapton was known have to take part in these Sunday happenings.

Rose Grove Railway Staff Club. Seated in the new staff club in 1962 are .(left to right) Jimmy Martin (Driver) Eric Laycock (station foreman and club chairman), Bill Hawkins (club steward), Bernard Warren (driver) and Guard G Hudson. By coincidence both the drivers here were involved in the same tragic accident up Copy Pit five years after this picture was taken. *Eric Laycock.*

Motive Power at Rose Grove.

Rose Grove was known for its large allocation of W.D. 2-8-0s. At one stage it was thought that only Wakefield shed had a larger allocation of these rough and ready workhorses. Quite often a number of the Wakefield engines could be seen working off the shed at Rose Grove covering local work whilst visiting the area and no doubt some of Rose Grove's would be doing the same in the Wakefield area. As many as 20 or so of the "Dug - Dees" would often be seen in the Rose Grove area at the same time. You either liked them or hated them. The ride was rough but they steamed like hell and the injectors were very reliable, quite easily able to keep up with the boiler. They were a common sight around the area for over twenty years, but I imagine that few people shed a tear when they moved off to pastures new at Langwith Junction and Colwick.

Local "Duggies" that seemed to stay in the area for many years included Nos.90040,90109, 90138, 90143, 90159, 90171, 90181, 90183, 90231, 90264, 90274,90314,90420, 90557.

When the local Austerity engines departed Rose Grove in 1965, ones from Wakefield and Normanton still continued to arrive in East Lancashire as late as the summer of 1967, though it is thought that the last one to travel over the route via Colne to Skipton was No.90404 of Wakefield depot on 16th June 1966, working the Burnley to Wath Road coal empties.

The "Crab" 2-6-0s did valiant service at Rose Grove, doing all manner of jobs from trip working to passengers and of course they were the mainstay of the motive power for the excursion traffic for many years throughout the 1950s and early 60s. The ones I recall are Nos.42706 42716, 42717,42828, 42869, 42898. All of these with one exception remained local until 1964 when they moved to Lower Darwen shed at Blackburn. The exception was No.42706 which was a 1963 withdrawal from Rose Grove. Other "Crabs" came and went, these included Nos.42901, 42926 and 42727, the latter was almost the last of the class to remain in service and, having spent some time at the Burnley shed, moved away to Stockport, eventually being withdrawn from Birkenhead shed in 1967.

Passenger tank engines were allocated to Rose Grove until 1963, when they moved away to Lostock Hall. Their work on the local passenger services had been taken over by diesel railcars in 1960 and '61. Those that readily spring to mind are Nos.42546, 42547 and 42555. Of these No.42546 remained in use locally until 1967 and was noted in temporary store at Colne carriage sheds in May of 1966.

The little 3F tank engines were the staple shunt engines at Rose Grove for many years, doing shunt and trip work at Burnley Central and Danes House yards as well as Manchester Road coal yard. They also shunted the hump yards at Rose Grove covering the Up Side shunt turn and the Yard and East shunt on the Down side. Amongst the regulars to be seen were Nos.47333, 47383,47577 and 47631.

The ex L. and Y. types were dwindling fast by the mid to late 1950s, the "Lanky" tanks such as Nos.50651,50652, 50653, 50655, which had worked the "Puffing Billy" between Colne and Blackburn until December 1956, had gone by the middle of 1957. The "A" class tender engines which had been the regular trip engines around the area for many years had all but gone by the end of the 50s, but at least No.52179 survived until August of 1960, providing the last local link with the former Lancashire and Yorkshire Railway. "A" engines that could be seen in the late 1950s at Rose Grove included Nos.52095 52179, 52319, 52369 and 52526.

On Shed. A last glimpse of the shed roads before we drop out of sight towards the West Junction. Long term resident of Rose Grove No.**42898**, in very good order almost fresh from the works sits amidst a group of W.D's. No.**42898** was a popular choice for excursion work, keep your eye out for her in the next volume. (below) Dropping down to the West signalbox the shed yard was lost behind the banking and the coaling plant etc. Jim Dean (the older) is at the regulator of No.**48410** preparing for a run up the bank to Hapton. *Dave Dyson / Bill Hurst.*

Black Fives were never seen in large numbers at Rose Grove until the early to mid 60s when they replaced the ageing "Crab" 2-6-0s. The ones we would see in the 1950s tended to be used on the London passenger workings to Stockport and the odd "Resi." to Blackpool. Engines which had a long association with the shed were Nos.44940, 44948, 44949, 45205 and 45216; of these No.45205 seemed to spend a fair share of its time in the summer months working the many local excursion trains to the Lancashire coast.

Rose Grove West Junction.

Our stay at Rose Grove was always too brief and as we didn't draw up here, we were soon on our way again. With a quick blast on the hooter, our driver would slip effortlessly out of the island platform at Rose Grove and drop down past the shed yard, the view of the shed roads and the turntable area was only really a quick glimpse as the large red bricked "Lanky coal hole" blocked much of our view as did the towering structure of the more modern coaling plant. By the time we had passed Rose Grove West signalbox close to the West Junction, the loco yard was high above us on the banking top and as our seaside special edged away round the curve leading onto the Padiham branch, we tended to settle down to relax and look through the spotting notes that dad had made. The curve round onto the Padiham line would enable us to have a final look at the rear of the shed at Rose Grove. The back wall of the shed and part of the side wall were visible and as always smoke could be seen rising through the roof vents. The rear of the shed contained a number of windows but we were too far away to tell what lay inside. The shed itself was on the bank top above the Leeds to Liverpool Canal and, down by the side of the shed there were always a number of stored locomotives. In the 1950s these would more often than not be the ex Lancashire and Yorkshire types as well as the odd " Austerity 2-8-0.

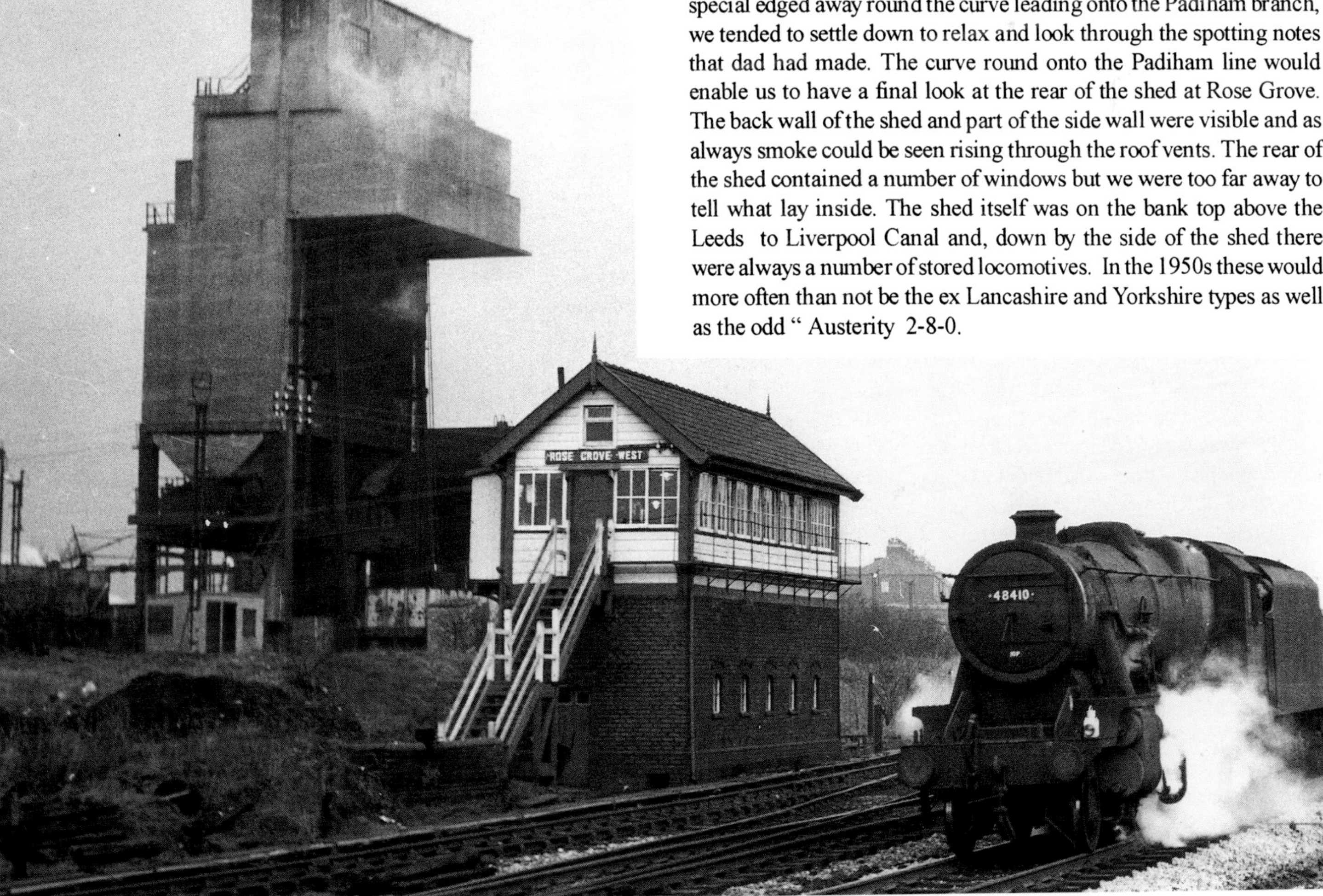

Round the "Padiham Loop"

Down to Padiham. Rose Grove's No.**42869** takes the Padiham loop line at Rose Grove West Junction with 1T80 the 10.27am Burnley to Blackpool Central period return on 1st July 1961. *John E Porter.*

Rose Grove West to Great Harwood via Padiham.

Taking the right hand signal at Rose Grove West Junction, we would cross the Leeds to Liverpool Canal once more and branching away to the right, we would leave the main line and begin the journey round the Padiham loop. Once over the junction points, it was surprising just how quickly the line began to fall on the steep gradient. Looking back from our position near to the loco., we would watch the non-corridor coaches of our train as they clattered over the junction one by one. More or less straight across from us as we took this wide sweeping curve, was the rear of Rose Grove shed and although it was some distance away we could clearly see the old engines stored down by the side of the shed. These were usually "Lanky" tanks and "A" class 0-6-0's all of which appeared to have sacks tied around their tall chimneys. In that era of change you could sense that somehow their working days were all over.

For the next minute or two we were treated to an elevated view across the broad valley. On both sides of the railway there were green fields and steep bankings. Looking ahead down the long straight section towards Padiham we could see a wide expanse of housing intermingled with mills and factories. Mill chimneys stood high above the rooftops of the houses, but few were smoking at the holidays. I remember thinking, why didn't they build their mills up here on the hillside, then at least the chimneys didn't need to be so tall! Well, at least I thought it made sense. The descent down the 1 in 40 bank was quite fast and as we approached the first of the housing, the rumble of the brake cylinders and rigging beneath our compartment told us that the driver was clearly "getting hold" of his train, steadying it up in readiness for the tight curve which would come with the run into Padiham station To give an impression of just how steep the incline was, as we passed the first rows of houses on the left side, we would be riding high on the banking top some 30 feet from ground level and we'd be looking out across the rooftops. Within seconds we would have dropped to bedroom window level and then down to ground floor height, all in a very short distance. By the time we reached the metal latticed footbridge which connected the two parts of Pendle Street, the houses running parallel to the line sported rather neat front gardens. From this point the line began curving away to the left , ready for the run into the station. Watching the trains go by seemed to be a local pastime for the people of Padiham, and why not ! There were always passers by who stopped in their tracks to look up towards us as we rolled by, high above them on the descent into Padiham. Children playing down by Russell Terrace, near to Dryden Street bridge, always waved and shouted at the trains and others playing close to the Pendle Street footbridge would make a mad dash to reach the footbridge before we passed beneath it. The long sweeping curve on the approach to Padiham station grew gradually tighter as we drifted round past Green Lane Mill. On the curve, we had a smashing view forward on our left side. We would watch the wheels and the motion of our engine revolving steadily round, the driver's face was a picture of concentration as he occasionally looked back in our direction and watched the rear of his train snake past the mills on the bend. His mate, holding on to the cab roof with one hand would be making the most of the downhill section to Padiham, soon he'd have to "Get some fire on" as drivers used to say, in readiness for the climb to Great Harwood. As we passed over Green Brook (river bridge), the goods yard connection branched away from the main line on the left side to travel over Station Road on a separate iron overbridge to the one used by the two main lines. Over here on the left side the large area of the goods yard at Padiham was situated. In the goods yard there was a large wooden goods warehouse ,a most unusual feature. It was quite unlike any other wooden warehouse structure we were likely to see on our travels by excursion train. Many of the goods yards that we would pass would have wooden extensions added to the main stone or brick shed but here at Padiham, the whole shed was made of timber and quite substantial it was too. This goods shed was positioned next to the goods loop which ran directly behind the Up side station buildings. A number of long sidings stretched out along the length of the yard and these were always full of "common users" coal wagons. As a rule there tended to be a locomotive shunting back and forth in the yard and more than likely it would be one of Rose Grove's Austerity 2-8-0's or a Crab. However I do recall seeing a little Stanier class 3 passenger tank at rest between shunt moves near the shunt neck by the platform on one of our trips, although this sort of occurrence was rare. To the rear of the goods yard a steep banking lead up to the boundary wall. Here on the hillside was a traditionally stone built Primary school or such, which was visible from the lineside which ever direction you were travelling on the railway. I often wondered as I looked up towards this point what superb views would be possible from such elevated classrooms.

At the foot of the 1in 40 Padiham bank, we quickly dropped from roof height down to garden level, close to Pendle Street footbridge. Here a Class 8 tackles the bank with empties from the power station.The small picture at the top is of No.**61875** of Hull Dairycoates shed, taken from the banking at Villiers Street in August 1960. It was working C208 the 8.10am Hull - Blackpool Central which ran between 9th July and 13 August 1960. *Brian Wrigglesworth, inset: Duncan Armstrong.*

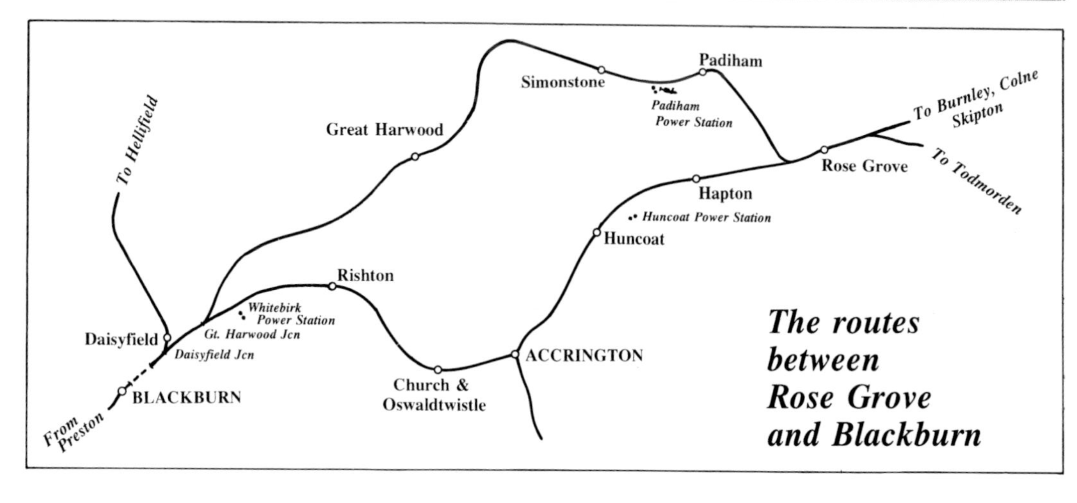

Padiham Green School. When young Duncan Armstrong watched trains from the Padiham Green School yard, this was the sort of view he would see, the railway ran on an embankment along the valley floor and the town of Padiham stretched out up the valley sides. *Duncan Armstrong.*

(below) **Padiham Station.** No.**42147** rolls round the curve into the platform at Padiham with a Blackburn bound train during the last week of local services on the line in October 1957. *John E Porter.*

Padiham Station. The way it looked in the 1920s. *(courtesy of Duncan Armstong).*

Padiham Station.

As a rule, upon entering Padiham, we'd be taking advantage of the curving view into the station and therefore we would miss the elevated outlook over the rooftops of the town centre, which was possible from over on the right side of the compartment. Also missed was Padiham's signal box which sat on the end of the Down side platform. Passing over the iron bridge above Station Road, into the platform, the tight curve there caused the coach wheels to give off a sort of ringing or hollow sound which echoed against the bridge wall. Possibly this was due to the fact that the wheels were solid rather than spoked. Soon a hoot from the engine whistle informed the waiting passengers of our approach. Entering the up platform you quickly became aware of the rundown state of the station, for example, the platform was covered in a carpet of green. Most of the platform surfaces were covered in grass of varying lengths, in fact only the area under the awnings seemed to be free from vegetation of one sort or another. Weeds and longer grass sat close by the old cast station sign which was mounted by the rear wall. The name "Padiham" was still proudly displayed but the paintwork on the sign which had once been a nice shiny red, was now just a faded shade of purple. The daily passenger service over the line had been withdrawn as from the 2nd December 1957, though the actual last train had run on the 30th November 1957. Despite the fact that the station was staffed after a fashion until well into the 1960s, there was little attempt to keep the weeds at bay, instead the Station Master and his men were busily employed in sorting out the many freight workings to the coal yard and the nearby power stations. Normally as we drifted through the platform, quite a large crowd would be anxiously looking in our direction, intent upon spotting the spare seats in the train and as we coasted to a stand at the platform end, a number of these day-trippers would be seen dashing along the grassy platform towards the carriages immediately in rear of ours. These enthusiastic excursionists would wrench open the carriage doors and, having found accommodation, they would shout back along the platform to where the rest of their family were standing, waving to them and urging them to come down to the front of the train. Rarely did anyone ever come up as far as the engine at Padiham. If the driver drew right to the platform end he could just nicely fit nine non-corridor coaches on the platform. We always ended up with our compartment close by the goods yard entrance and we were treated to some smashing views over on the right side of the compartment, up towards the Memorial Park at Padiham. The whole area was covered in mature shrubs and trees, beyond which lay a number of pathways surrounded by some really colourful flower beds. The whole area looked a picture in the bright summer sun. Situated at the top of the park was the Unitarian Church with its tall spire which stood out as a local landmark. It's funny, but in those days you tended to remember things such as church spires and mill chimneys, possibly because there were such a lot of them. Over at the station, the main office buildings were down below platform level, looking more like the frontage of a public house rather than a station. All the buildings throughout the station area were of dressed stone and the solid stone structure "down below" comprised the booking hall and general waiting room, together with some offices. A long subway ran beneath the two main lines and it was connected to the platforms by steep slopes with flag floors. The walls of the subway were just bare dressed stone. The first floor of the main station building contained the station house, which had a separate entrance via an elevated walkway. The dismal facilities provided for passengers over the years must clearly have aided in driving potential customers away from the railway at Padiham. Up on the platforms themselves the same quality of dressed stone prevailed. On the Down platform there were ladies and gents waiting rooms, toilets etc. together with a lamp room and porters accommodation and the station masters office. Over on the Up side the buildings there were somewhat smaller, just ladies and gents waiting rooms being provided. Awnings covered only a small area of the platform and as mentioned earlier, it was only these parts of the platform which appeared to be kept free of grass and weeds. Padiham seemed to escape the era of the B.R. "sausage" sign and in consequence I can't recall any enamel signs on the station at all. The various signs relating to the waiting rooms etc. were still of the wood frame type with mounted lettering. The paintwork again was very tarnished and faded.

The river separated us from the hillside leading up to the Memorial park and as we departed from Padiham we would pass over the river bridge on our way towards the twin power stations of Padiham "A" and "B". Upon our return from the seaside a set of Rose Grove men would be patiently sat on their old Crab loco. near to the river bridge ready to give us a push up the bank to Rose Grove, but for now our thoughts were clearly upon the journey ahead through the delightful Lancashire countryside and as far as we were concerned, the journey home was a long way off yet......

Empty Platform. It certainly wasn't like this at the holiday times. The grassy platform at Padiham would be crowded with eager daytrippers during the July holidays. No.**42147** awaits departure from Padiham in October 1957.
John E Porter.

Padiham Goods Yard.
Rose Grove's No.**90420** shunts round the back of the station in Padiham's goods yard. *Duncan Armstrong.*

Two and one half to "Lew - in - gruel"

Young Duncan Armstrong of Padiham always had a close affection for the railway that passed through the town. In the summer months when the line became a busy diversionary route for excursion traffic he would often rush from his Shakespeare Street home to the railway embankment at the end of the street to watch the many specials as they descended Padiham bank. When the local Burnley holidays came around, (Padiham's were also at this time), Duncan's family in keeping with a great many other local folk would head off for their holidays using the train and sometimes, the Armstrong family holiday would be taken at some quiet out of the way place, one such holiday involved travelling to the Cambrian Coast town of Llwyngwril. The idea was to use the "Penychain", the Butlin's holiday train, travelling on it as far as Afonwen and it was here after reaching the Cambrian Coast route that this particular service reversed to head towards Pwllheli and the Butlins camp at Penychain. The Armstrong family would then catch a service train down the coast to Llwyngwril, which was 2 miles south of Fairbourne, on the other side of estuary from Barmouth.

Duncan had offered to nip down to the station at Padiham to obtain tickets for the journey, which incidentally would start from Rose Grove rather than Padiham as the Penychain train always travelled via Accrington. Tickets were however still available from Padiham booking office for the train. Duncan, quite excited by thought of the forthcoming trip, set off for the station on the eve of the holidays. It was here that the problems started because Duncan can at times sound to have a very broad Lancashire accent and the holiday destination of Llwyngwril as pronounced by Duncan sounds more like "Lew - in - gruel".

As Duncan presented himself at the ticket office window, it became apparent that the be-spectacled man behind the counter was already somewhat harassed.

The booking office had not seen regular staff since 1957, when the local services ended, and a booking clerk was only provided for the holidays trains at Easter, Whitsuntide and the general holidays. It was always a case of being thrown in at the deep end for these relief booking clerks. "Two and one half to Lew - in - gruel" announced Duncan as the clerk peered at him through the booking office window. For a moment or two the booking clerk went into a trance as he obviously tried the place mentally where this destination was. Out came a map which was quickly spread out on the desk top. Judging by Duncan's pronunciation of Lew - in - gruel, the booking clerk must have thought the "Lew " bit referred to Looe as in Cornwall and Duncan watched amused as the clerk slowly manoeuvred his finger around the Cornish coastline looking for the resort. "It's in Wales" shouted Duncan, "I know, I know" replied the harassed clerk, his finger suddenly jerking up the map to the Welsh coast. Still perusing the map, the booking clerk raised his head up from the map and looking over his spectacles towards Duncan's smiling face he commented "with getten some good trips to Blackpool tha nose". "I know" said Duncan "but wid much sooner guter Lew - in - gruel". Thankfully the clerk did eventually find the fare scale and the tickets were duly booked so all that remained was to ensure that ample time was allowed for the journey from Padiham to Rose Grove in order to catch the 8.16 am departure to North Wales the following morning.

On another occasion there must have been a rush to put up the excursion posters in the windows above the booking office lobby as the one advertising Morecambe was pasted on the window upside down .....!

The large crowds that lined the little platforms at Padiham during the local holidays are well remembered by Duncan, as are the odd funny happenings.

One holiday as Duncan and his parents waited on the busy platform for a excursion train to Blackpool, a number of local people were across on the Down side waiting for the seven minutes past eight train up to Rose Grove. As the local service drew in to the station one well known local character, Admiral Dewhurst (his name not his rank) leaned out of the window of the non - corridor compartment to talk to some of the crowd on the other platform. Another well known man, Rueben McClainer shouted across to him "Get thee heyd in, thill think its a cattle truck". The Admiral, who was clearly not amused by the outburst quickly drew the window up as the train eased out of the platform

View from the Park. From the Memorial park at Padiham looking across to the railway we would see the goods yard and high on the hill Padiham Green School. Bank engines would wait in the evening by the river bridge here to assist the specials up to Rose Grove. *Duncan Armstrong.*

(below-right). **"Runaway"** No not Del Shannon's hit record of 1961, more a case of No.**90511** hitting the dead end of the power station sidings at Padiham "B". Having runaway down the bank the signalman inadvertantly turned the coal train into the sidings and the WD almost made it up on to the main road to Altham. Driver Ted Shackleton and his mate emerged "Shaken but not stirred" ......! *Leo Moore.*

Padiham Power Stations and the line to Great Harwood Junction.

Beyond the river bridge, there were sidings which branched away to the left, into the C.E.G.B. power stations of Padiham "A" &"B". These long reception and storage sidings would contain a considerable amount of coal traffic. Padiham "A" st. tion had been in operation since before the 2nd World War and in the late 1950s work commenced upon the construction of the Padih um "B" plant. From around 1957 until 1960, we had watched the nev power plant grow from a piece of spare land to a massive complex with two huge 300 feet high cooling towers capable of handling 3.5 million gallons of water per hour. These cooling towers sat very close to the railway in comparison to many other power stations. The large turbine hall and the boiler houses stood close together with the chimney which was even higher than the cooling towers. The whole project cost twelve million pounds, which was quite a lot of money at the time. Our days of travelling over the Padiham loop line were almost over by the time the Padiham "B" station became fully operational. The power station was a familiar landmark to us and it could be seen for miles and quite easily from down the valley in the Blackburn direction near Martholme etc. Moving on past the power station our excursion train pulled away under the main Altham road and for a short distance to Simonstone we would travel in shallow cuttings. The tiny station at Simonstone was quickly passed as the driver accelerated towards Martholme. The disused platforms at Simonstone were overgrown, for like Padiham, the station had closed on the 2nd of December 1957. Unlike Padiham and Great Harwood, which still catered for holiday traffic, no passengers would ever again alight here. The goods yard was still occupied by a local coal merchant and the wooden goods shed was still to be seen standing behind the Up platform. The irony behind the withdrawal of local passenger services was that some 12 months prior to closure, the new Mullard television tube factory which was set to employ in the region of 400 workers had approached the railway management in the hope that they would re-time the first train from Blackburn in a morning by ten minutes; this would allow a fair percentage of the Mullard staff to travel by train. The railways reply was to amend the 1956 timetable so that the first passenger train out of Blackburn didn't even call at Simonstone ......!

After Simonstone, except for one overbridge, we would be riding on a small embankment all the way to Martholme and the views were superb! The valley opened up to reveal some beautiful Lancashire countryside and it was a scene which became more dazzling the nearer to Martholme we travelled. Lush green meadows would be seen, with cows and sheep grazing lazily in them. Farmers would be busy baling hay, using an assortment of old machinery. Few farmers in those days had modern tractors, relying heavily on the old David Brown "Cropmaster" and the little grey "Ferguson" of the post war years. Baling machines quite often had been converted from horse drawn vehicles and as we passed these scenes of hectic activity the smell of the newly baled hay wafted in through the open compartment window. The driver would shut off steam as we approached Martholme. It was a curved approach to the viaduct there and on this wide sweeping curve of the valley side, the vista was magnificent. On over the viaduct we rolled, to our left the whole of the valley was to be seen right along to Padiham power station and even beyond that point towards Burnley, what a picture it all looked in the bright summer sun! The right hand view at Martholme was one which lead across to the rolling hills close to Whalley, beyond which lay the delights of the Ribble valley. The dressed stone viaduct at Marthholme was extremely

continued on page 69

(above). **Simonstone Station.** This delightful scene of a rural stopping train service would be a thing of the past at Simonstone shortly after this picture was taken in 1957. Not even the excursions would call here after that date. No.**76082** arrives from Blackburn, heading for Rose Grove. *John E Porter.*

(below). **Martholme Viaduct.** Having curved right round the valley, it was at Martholme Viaduct that we were treated to this glorious view back along to Padiham, by the 1960s the new Padiham "B" plant dominated the skyline. *S.Taylor.*

Running into Great Harwood

1Z12 Colne - Southport. 15.4.63. You can fairly hear the exhaust from No.**42828** as it climbs up the bank from Heys Lane into Great Harwood station on Easter Monday 1963. (note the steam heat). *Geoff Robinson.*

continued from page 67

well built, designed to last for years but sadly within a few short summers the last excursion trains would have pounded over the high arches of Martholme viaduct and no more would we be treated to those classic views from the train. The climb up to Great Harwood was quite stiff, made somewhat harder by the driver having eased off for the curve on the approach to Marthholme viaduct. Once over the viaduct he would hoist the regulator into "second valve" and drop the reversing wheel forward to climb the 1 in 90 to Heys Lane. On the climb up to Great Harwood it was unlikely that the reverser would be pulled back beyond 45 %, the load behind the engine usually being nine non - corridor coaches. With our engine clearly "shouting the odds", we would pass by the closed Martholme colliery where once a small signal box had stood and where derelict overgrown sidings now lay. Over to the right just after the colliery, the golfers on the fairways of Great Harwood golf links could be seen to turn and look up towards us as their game was interrupted by the roar of the engine as we rattled on up the embankment. The distant signal at "Harrod" East signalbox must have been in the off position as the driver "dropped the gear", giving his engine "the works" for the run up through Great Harwood. Ahead the gasometers to our right some distance away indicated that the station was just around the bend and still climbing, though not just as steeply at this point, we'd pass Heys Lane. It was here that the gasworks yard and the sidings of the goods yard came into view on our right hand side. The goods yard was of considerable size as was the goods warehouse itself and it was in this very busy yard that a great percentage of the produce and raw materials involved with the local textile industry had been transhipped in years gone by. Great Harwood had 22 cotton mills within its town boundaries at one stage and 14 pubs together with 13 clubs, how's that for working hard and playing hard......!

Great Harwood Goods Yard, Carriage Shed and Station Area.

The goods yard could easily handle 80 wagons or more and there was a busy coal and coke trade relating to domestic and mill coal together with the gasworks requirements. From Heys Lane on the left side of the railway the extensive carriage sheds sidings would cover a large area right up past the station towards the Albert Street bridge. The carriage sheds had been a important repair and maintenance depot with cleaning facilities etc. in the immediate post war years, however the 1950s had seen the closure of this facility and by the end of the decade the sidings were disused and the carriage shed was falling into decay. Latterly rows of condemned stock occupied the sidings before all the staff were withdrawn. Once the sheds were un-manned it was felt unwise to stable stock in the area for any length of time, even the condemned variety. Great Harwood East signal cabin was positioned on the Down side near to the goods yard and across from the carriage sheds. Almost next to the signalbox was a small loading dock. Passing this point, if you looked across to the right you could see the little engine shed over in the nearby gasworks yard. Ahead of us as our loco. blasted its way up the slightly easing gradient of 1 in 102 lay the short station platforms at Great Harwood. Only 5 coaches would fit on either platform and should we have called here, which occasionally we did, then drawing up would most certainly have been the order of the day. The station buildings like those at Padiham were of dressed stone and the design of the main buildings which were situated upon the Down platform was again not unlike that of the Down side buildings at Padiham. The station masters office had a bay window in which was situated a clock, just like the one at Padiham. Ladies and gents waiting rooms and toilet facilities were provided as was the porters room etc. and a sizeable awning ran for some length along the platform face. The Up side buildings were however somewhat spartan, the awning having been removed from the small waiting room some time before the station ceased to cater for local travellers. A metal latticed footbridge, similar to the one at Rishton station a few miles away, connected the two platforms and a parachute water tank sat at the end of the Up platform near to the very large brick built lamp-room which was situated down by the lineside beyond the platform end.

The gradient eased still further to 1 in 196 as we pounded up through the deserted station platforms, the sound of the engine had as usual, brought forth a number of children from the nearby streets around by Railway Terrace and as our train climbed steadily past Great Harwood West signal box, these enthusiastic youngsters would be seen sitting on the wall top and on the grassy embankment near to the signalbox and they would shout and wave until we disappeared in a cloud of smoke through Unity Bridge.

Geoff Robinson, seen here with son Michael, thankfully made sure those last summer specials over the branch were recorded for posterity.

Eric Laycock has many happy memories of working trains in and out of the Great Harwood carriage sheds, but on one occasion , there was little to smile about..........

Whilst he was involved on the seasonal carriage shunting work in the mid 1950s, a shunt was required at Harwood to release a BSK coach which was sat on the blocks behind another 19 coaches. Eric was ably assisted as always by Frank Bairstow. Frank drew out the whole of the 20 coaches using their WD 2-8-0. He dropped off the train some distance up the line between the Unity Bridge and the one at Meadow Street, in order to see Eric as he stood on the Down main line ready to stop the lengthy train once it was clear of the shed sidings. Eric duly waved to Frank to stop and, having pulled the points for the front loop, he then waved to the ever-willing Bairstow, in an attempt to get the train eased up for uncoupling. This was followed by another wave to Frank to get the driver to "Tap" the now uncoupled coach down the loop. This is the bit Eric would rather not remember. Before he could climb aboard to wind the brake on, the coach ran away on him and careered down the loop towards Great Harwood East signalbox, where the bewildered signalman could do little only watch as the coach headed past at speed. At the end of the loop the stop-block was made of concrete, which succeeded in stopping the leading bogie of the coach, but the coach body continued on - coming to rest overhanging Heys Lane. Apparently a picture appeared in the local press of a Ribble bus passing gingerly beneath the pivoting coach body that sat high above on the railway banking.

Great Harwood Station. After 1957 the only trains to call at Great Harwood were the specials at Easter Whitsuntide and the holiday fortnight in late July. Arriving from Padiham No.**45205** enters the station with 1T65 a Padiham - Blackpool excursion on Saturday 21st July 1962. *Geoff Robinson.*

Seaside specials at Great Harwood

1T95 to Southport. No.**42732** almost fresh out of Horwich works (June 1962) prepares to collect stock from the nearby carriage sheds to work to Southport on 21st July 1962. *Geoff Robinson.*

1T65 to Blackpool. This Blackburn holidays excursion of 21st July 1962 is seen departing out of the station at Great Harwood, next stop will be Blackburn. The aptly named Railway View is over the wall behind No.**45205**, which incidentally was one of Rose Grove' s best Black 5's. *Geoff Robinson.*

Almost the end of an era

1T58 to Blackpool. Setting out for Blackburn on a rather dull day No.**44728** heads towards Unity Bridge, which as usual is lined with children etc. watching the seaside departures. The time of day was 11.25am and 1T58 was the 11.15am Rose Grove - Blackpool Central excursion on Whit Monday 18th May 1964. This was one of the last trains ever to call at Great Harwood. *Geoff Robinson.*

" Blackpool Bound." Great Harwood just the way we remember it, Black 5's non-corridor stock, rows of terraced houses, the odd church spire and kids .... yes lots of waving children. When the sound of an engine whistle was heard in Harwood children would come running down to Railway View and onto the Unity Bridge. What a sad day it must have been when these holiday specials ceased running in 1964. 3T46, really 1T46 had called at Great Harwood station on Monday 27th July 1964 and was now climbing away up through the cutting towards the bridge that led to the Unity field and further on still it would pass beneath Meadow Street bridge which gave access to the Palatine and Devron mills that were situated next to the railway banking. Soon driver Johnny McManus on Rose Grove's No.**44949** would roll over the top of the bank at Lidgett Bridge, then it would be a steady run into Blackburn. (below left) Johnny McManus is seen the next day, Tuesday 28th July 1964, again with No.**44949**, this time on a Morecambe excursion 1Z22, passing over Lidgett Bridge at the top of the bank from Great Harwood. In the background is the chimney of Palatine Mill. Over to the left of the picture are the houses along the main road from Harwood to Rishton. The Blackburn and Great Harwood holidays of 1964 would be the last time that trains called at Great Harwood station and by 1964 only a select few were booked to call. Finally (below right) sitting on the school wall at the corner of Vicar Street and School Street in Great Harwood we see a group of the youngsters who, upon hearing a whistle, would dash to Railway View, they include Michael Robinson (extreme left) and (far right) Mary and John Robinson, the picture as you may have guessed is by Father Geoff Robinson as are the

Bernard Bond who lived in Great Harwood during the 1950s and 60s, made notes of a number of the special workings that travelled over the North Lancashire loop (better known locally as the Padiham Loop) and these notes are listed here, they show the locomotives seen, together with their shed allocations at the time.

Saturday 9th July 1960 (Saturday at the start of the second week of Colne's annual holiday)
61010 (50B) 42727 (27B) 45104 (26A) 42794 (41B) 45601 (26A) 42938 (9A) 42455 (24E)
44709 (24L) 44958 (12A) 42468 (26F) 42828 (24B) 75016 (27C) 42842 (24F) 45230 (24L)
44525 (6G) 42557 (27D) 61110 (56B) 42869 (24B).

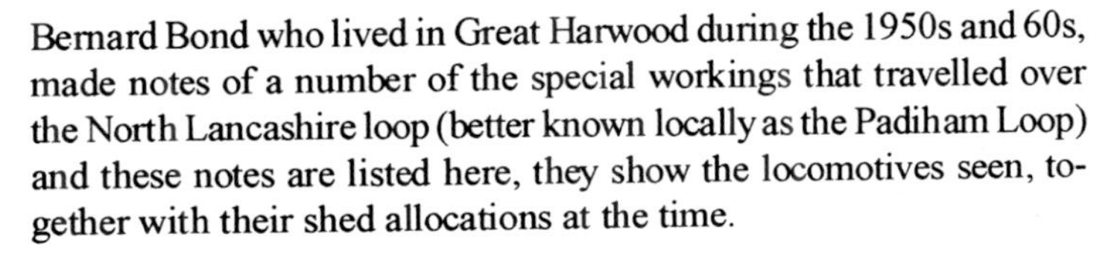

Sunday 10th July 1960
73161 (55E) 45695 (55C) 48357 (56D) 42869 (24B) 90407 (55C) 45108 (8F) 42869 (24B)
61289 (50B) 44912 (56F) 42317 (8F) 44696 (26A) 90181 (24B) 42303 (8F) 90614 (62A) 61270 (36A)

A date in September 1960 believed to be Saturday 24th.
73160 (55E) 42547 (24B) 61015 (56A) 92078 (18A) 90143 (24B) 90238 (18B) 61030 (51A) 61812 (36A) 73000 (41B) 61893 (50B) 90635 (56A) 90517 (51L).

Whit Sunday 21st May 1961
(locos. listed together with shed allocations and the time they were seen).
42718 (24D) 8am 42732 (24D) 8.13am 42719 (26D) 8.19am 45265 (21A) 8.50am 44937 (9A) 9.12am 42483 (24D) 9.35am 42703 (24E) 10.15am 90376 (26A) 10.17am 76084 (24D) 10.34am 45209 (24B) 10.40am 44937 (5A) 10.44am 40126 (6A) 11.20am (this loco. had apparently come north from the Somerset and Dorset line to Chester and was now working from Bolton for the last few days of its working life, prior to scrapping at Horwich). 44778 (24E) 11.40am 44987 (26B) 12.05pm 45205 (24B) 12.15pm 61201 (26B)

The Padiham to Great Harwood loop line would remain open for excursion traffic also freights, empty stock trains and light engines etc. until the end of the 1964 summer season.
The last excursion trains to call at Padiham would be the Colne and Nelson local holiday specials, during the two weeks in July, commencing Saturday 6th. The last excursion trains to call at Great Harwood would be those which traversed the loop line over the Whitsuntide period. These were **1T52**, the 11am Colne to Blackpool Central on Saturday 16th May, the loco. was Rose Grove's 44949, on Whit Sunday **1Z12**, the 10.20am Colne to Southport Chapel Street, **1T64**, 11.17am Burnley Central to Blackpool Central, the loco. was a Rose Grove engine 44940 and **1T81**, which was the 11.56am Colne to Fleetwood excursion, the loco. was Rose Grove's 45205. Whit Monday would see the final two services to call, **1T58** which was the 11.15am Rose Grove to Blackpool Central and **1Z12** which formed the 11.42am Colne to Southport excursion.

Excursion Workings from Great Harwood

Whit Sunday and whit Monday, 10th and 11th June 1962.

1962 would almost certainly be the last year that coaching stock was stabled at Great Harwood carriage sidings in readiness for excursion workings which essentially started at Blackburn. In the 1950s, the carriage sheds at Harwood played a key part in the holiday traffic arrangements, cleaning watering and repairs were all carried out at this busy little depot. Stock was ferried to and from from Colne in order to cover the many summer workings.

By the mid 50s the carriage sheds were in decline and the dawning of the 1960s would see the shed as a storage point for condemned coaching stock, in the pre-Beeching purge. The roof was removed and by 1962 only the main walls remained standing, but the lengthy carriage shed roads were still intact and therefore they were still used at the busy holiday periods to store stock for Blackburn area excursions. Coaching stock for these various specials would be tripped into Great Harwood during the week prior to the events from Lostock Hall or Colne carriage sheds..

10/6/62

	A	A	A	A	A									
	Halifex to Blackpool Cen. (76083)	Halifex to Blackpool Cen.	Halifex to Llandudno	Halifex to Southport	Halifex Settle to Blackpool Cen.	Garex Ossett								
	1T65	1T85	1T84	1Z15	1T83	1X3								
COLNE .... arr	..	9 56	9 39	..	..	..								
.... dep	..	9 58	9 41	..	..	..								
Nelson	..	10 3	9 46	..	..	..								
Brierfield	..	10 7	9 50	..	..	..								
BURNLEY CEN. arr	..	..	9 56	..	..	..								
dep	..	10 12	9 57	..	..	..								
Burnley Barracks........	..	..	10 0	..	..	..								
Rose Grove East.... arr	..	..	..	..	..	..							..	..
.... dep	..	..	..	..	..	..					..	..	..	..
Rose Grove............	..	10 15	10 5	..	..	..			..	10 34	10 49	..	10 48	11 2
Padiham	..	10 19	..	..	..	..	..	10 36	..	..	10 53	..	..	..
Great Harwood.......	..	..	..	..	..	..	..	10 44	..	..	..	..	..	..
Church	..	..	10 20	SL	..	FL	..	..						
Rishton	..	..	10 25	..	..	..	..	..						
BLACKBURN .... arr	..	..	10K31	..	10 45	..	..	..						
.... dep	10 28	10 35	10K41	..	10 47	..	..	10 54						

1T65 to Blackpool. (3T65 ex-Great Harwood) passes Bradkirk near Kirkham on Whit Sunday 10th June 1962. *Peter Fitton.*

1Z11 The 10.23 Burnley Central to Southport called at Great Harwood at 10.44am.

The sequence of events at Great Harwood on Sunday 10th June are as follows. Three sets of stock were stabled at Harwood and one set had been stored at Greenbank sidings, at Great Harwood Junction

0T64 Light engine from Rose Grove to Great Harwood to collect stock to work **1T64** Blackburn to Llandudno (depart light engine. Rose Grove 8.5am, depart Great Harwood for Blackburn at 8.50am to work to Llandudno at 9.15am. (The reason for Rose Grove covering this job was because of route knowledge, Harry Veevers and Tommy Kelly etc. being amongst the Rose Grove men who signed the North Wales Coast).

3T70 Loco. No.**42838** departed Great Harwood C.sheds for Darwen at 8.50 am, to work via Bolton Johnson Street, and pick up at Chorley etc. en-route to Blackpool Central.

3T65 Loco. No.**76083** departed Great Harwood carriage sheds for Blackburn at 10.05am, to work the 1028am. to Blackpool Central.

3Z10 was the 11.22am departure from Great Harwood Junction; to work the 11.30am Blackburn to Southport special **1Z10**.

1T71 The 10.55am Earby to Morecambe Promenade called at Great Harwood at 11.36am.

1T67 The 11.37am Colne to Blackpool Central (loco.No.**42717**) passed Great Harwood at 11.58am having called only at Padiham.

1T69 The 11.50am Colne to Fleetwood (loco.No.**42898**) called at Great Harwood at 12.29pm.

In the evening, the stock stabled overnight at Harwood was **3Z10** which arrived back at Great Harwood Jnc. at 7.55pm, again stabled at Greenbank Gas Sidings, whilst at Great Harwood itself, **3T65** arrived at 8.25pm and **3T70** arrived back at 8.55pm, the last arrival being the return Llandudno special **3T64**, the loco. going light to Rose Grove. No doubt the Grove men were "short resting" as this was a Sunday.

Whit Monday 11th June 1962.
1Z10 The 9am Colne to Southport called at Great Harwood at 9.35am.

3T67 Loco.No.**42728** worked the 10.25am from Great Harwood Junction to Darwen, to work **1T67** to Blackpool via Chorley.

3T62 Loco.No.**42733** departed Great Harwood at 10.35am for Blackburn, to work the 10.55am to Blackpool Central.

3T63 Loco.No.**42838** departed Great Harwood at 11.11am for Blackburn to work the 11.30am to Blackpool Central.

1T71 Loco.No.**45205,** the 11.15am Padiham to Blackpool Central, called at Great Harwood at 11.23am.

3T65 Loco.No.**42718** departed Great Harwood at 11.50am for Blackburn, to work the 12.10pm to Blackpool Central.

1Z13 The 11.25am Colne to Southport called at Great Harwood at 12.04pm.

3T64 Loco.No.**76084** departed Great Harwood at 1.30pm, to work the 1.45pm from Blackburn to Blackpool Central.

There was also a **1T61** special from Blackburn to Morecambe at 11.08am using loco. No.**45464** which came as **3T61** from Lostock Hall carriage sidings at 10.40am.

The return specials on the Monday evening **1T62** (No.**42752**), (note the change of engine here), **1T63** (No.**42838**), **1T64** (No.**76084**), were again stabled at Great Harwood, the locomotives together with the engine off **1T67**, (No.**42728**) which had deposited its train at Greenbank Gas Sidings, all ran light to Lower Darwen. The return special via Great Harwood to Padiham, **1T71**, with loco. No.**45205**, continued on to Colne to stable the coaching stock, before running light to its home depot of Rose Grove.

A number of overbridges would be passed whilst journeying through Great Harwood and all along this section of line we were travelling in a fairly deep cutting, the gradient again increasing to 1 in 90. Around us were mills to the left and terraced houses to the right, even the odd church spire prevailed yet again and once the cemetery came into view upon our right side, then we knew that just around the corner we'd be leaving the sights and sounds of "Harrod" far behind. ("Harrod" being the local term for Great Harwood). The gradient eased considerably upon passing the cemetery, the 1 in 90 became more like 1 in 250 as we rounded the curve on the approach to Tottleworth Bridge (Lidgett Bridge) and soon the cuttings and curves would bring us past the main road bridge to Rishton. From here it was down hill to Great Harwood Junction and back onto the main line once more. We never grew tired of the run over the "loop". In the height of the summer it was a pleasure to behold, the local townsfolk seemed so cheery, it was just like a country branch line .....!
The journey down to the junction was uneventful, but no doubt restful for the young fireman. The locos. safety valves sizzled merrily and the young lad could be seen hanging out of the cab watching the water pump take hold as he topped up the boiler. Soon the Leeds to Liverpool Canal joined us once more and high on the horizon stood the great "Metropolis" of Blackburn. Rows of terraced houses, with smoky chimneys and factory after factory covered the distant hills, all were sat in a murky sort of haze that grew nearer and nearer all the time.
Great Harwood Junction was reached in fine style and we rolled gently along the shallow cutting near to the modern Whitebirk industrial estate, coming to rest at the junction home signal.

"Ringo" Beatlemania must surely have been in full swing as Geoff Robinson snapped passing excursion 1Z32 with Derby engine No.**45684** *Jutland* at the head. In his notebook Geoff wrote 45684 , *"Ringo"* down by the date. Clearly chalked on the nameboard was Ringo. So what was No.**45684** doing on the Harwood loop line? Well, she had worked a Bloxwich to Blackpool special 1T80, then failed at the seaside resort. Once repaired it was "borrowed" to work to Colne, after which Rose Grove turned it out to work a Special from Colne to Lakeside on Sunday 26th July 1964 and on Tuesday the 28th it almost caught Geoff off guard as it rolled through Norden bridge working 1Z32 a Blackburn holidays special to Morecambe. *Geoff Robinson.*

Travelling via Accrington

"**Choppin Them Off**" (Gypsy Bridge 17.7.65.) No.**75027** is making light work of the climb to Hapton with the 11.16am S.O. Colne to Southport. Above the engines exhaust is the rear of Rose Grove shed and hidden by the banking on the left is the line to Padiham.
Noel Coates.

Rose Grove West to Accrington.

When looking at this route to Accrington and on to Blackburn, it is as well to point out that few of the excursions originating from Colne would actually travel via Accrington whilst the Padiham Loop remained open for through traffic. Nearly all the Blackpool bound excursions went via Padiham as did the Lakeside and Barrow coast specials, also the Llandudno period return trains. Some of the North Wales day trips which would include destinations such as Llandudno, would however travel via Accrington and Baxenden Bank, calling at Ramsbottom and Bury en route. The Southport's would travel over both routes, there was always a close affinity between Accrington and Southport and a number of booked services ran on a regular basis via Accrington from both Colne and Todmorden. At Colne holidays therefore it was somewhat of a novelty to use the Accrington route. It was only after the 1964 holidays when summer trains ceased to travel via Padiham that the journey round by Accrington became familiar to us. Heading away from Rose Grove, it was a steady climb to Hapton and upon leaving Rose Grove West Junction and passing over the Leeds to Liverpool canal, the first overbridge was known as Gypsy Bridge. This was an ideal location from which to watch the trains go by and from the photographers point of view, the climb away from Rose Grove would usually see the engines working hard. Quite often in the summertime especially at the holidays, groups of spotters could be seen as we approached this point. It was also ideal because just down the lane from Gypsy Bridge was the other overbridge which spanned the Padiham line and some photographers armed with a special traffic notice would be able to check which excursions were travelling over which route. On many occasions as we passed through the cutting on the approach to Gypsy bridge, we would watch the photographers quickly snap our picture and then start to dash towards the lane as they headed off to the Padiham line overbridge in order to get ready for the next excursion train. Beyond Gypsy Bridge the line ran almost straight to Hapton station and ahead of us the tall cooling towers of Huncoat Power Station dominated the skyline. From the top of the twin cooling towers, billowing white clouds would drift steadily upwards into the bright blue sky. In later years the new Padiham "B" Power Station would become just as familiar a landmark as Huncoat and in the early 1960s on the run up to Huncoat we would be able to see both sets of cooling towers busily sending forth their sulphurous clouds along the valley, incidentally on a clear day from the top road between Colne and Nelson both Huncoat and Padiham "B" Power Stations could clearly be seen.

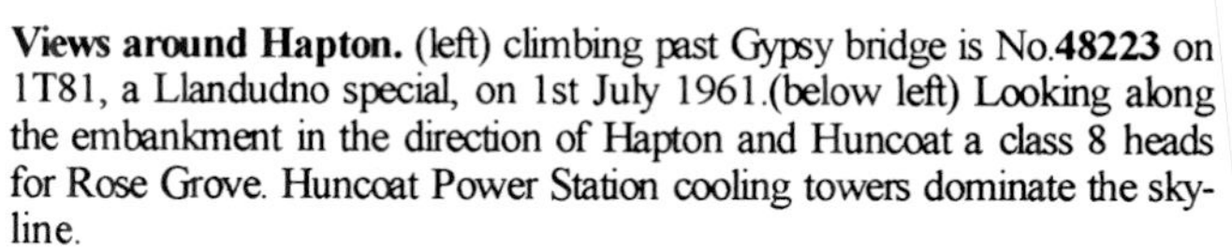

Views around Hapton. (left) climbing past Gypsy bridge is No.**48223** on 1T81, a Llandudno special, on 1st July 1961.(below left) Looking along the embankment in the direction of Hapton and Huncoat a class 8 heads for Rose Grove. Huncoat Power Station cooling towers dominate the sky-line.

(above and below) are two views at Hapton signalbox, the lower one shows Accrington fireman Mark Marshall's father-in-law, signalman Danny Dean. *John E Porter, Eddie Bobrowski and Mark Marshall.*

Hapton Station. The two views here show the neat surroundings of Hapton, a place rarely called at by our seaside specials. Above, a well turned out Class 4 enters the Up platform with a local passenger train. These services were invariably Accrington based engines and men who handled workings out as far as Skipton and Manchester. The picture below, again of a local passenger train, shows the view in the direction of Accrington with one of the cooling towers of Huncoat power station to the extreme left. This Fairburn variation of the 2-6-4T loco was also an Accrington (24A) based engine. Although BR enamel signs had made an appearance, much existed which provided evidence of the station's ancestry. Platform furniture, fittings, and signs still bore their L & Y hallmark, as did the entrance at road level. The platforms themselves had undergone reconstruction by utilizing standardized concrete components from Newton heath and "gardens" had been formed at the base of the embankments, making efficient use of 'half' barrels for "planters".

J.E. Porter

Hapton station.

The little station at Hapton was our next passing point. There was always a busy coal yard here situated on the right opposite the signal box, which was just before the station overbridge. Once through the bridge hole the narrow platforms and the small but adequate station buildings came into view. Rarely did we stop here, even though it was the local holidays. Some of the Sunday excursions to Southport etc. would call at all these little places and as usual, drawing up would be required. One interesting feature of the station overbridge was that beneath the blackened arch, mounted on the wall was a template of the bridge arch made in wood, with which the engineers could regularly check the gauge of the arch. No doubt this was a result of Hapton Valley Colliery being situated beneath the railway at this point. Sadly, Hapton always gave the air of being rundown long before staff were withdrawn in the 1960's. Once beyond Hapton we would climb steadily round the curve leading to Huncoat, the power station sidings to be seen on the right side of the line as we approached the power station and a modern British Railways design of signal box controlling movements to and from the sidings. The signal box was calle Huncoat Power Station and shiny red enamel name-boards wer mounted on the signal box gable ends as was the fashion with th later B.R. signal boxes. The huge structure of the power station, th cooling towers, turbine hall and boiler houses sat some distance awa high on the banking to the left of the railway.

The power plant at Huncoat was quite modern in the 1950s and th exchange sidings were always full of coal wagons. These sidings wer re-modelled in later years and modern fireless engines, nicknam "thermos flasks" provided the shunting power. Coal was transferr to the power plant by large overhead conveyers which transport the coal high above both main lines and across to the storage poi near the plant. Huge stockpiles of coal were constantly being turn over by a number of bulldozers emblazoned with the letters C.E.G.B. The large stockpiles spilled almost down to the lane close by the rai way and like molten lava the coal appeared to be constantly on th move.

Power Station Sidings. No.**90318** of Wakefield clanks steadily past the Huncoat power station sidings in the early 1960s.Extensively remodelled over the years these sidings would hold thousands of wagons, the coal from which was transferred by conveyer to a point behind the camera, where it was constantly kept turning by bulldozers. *Duncan Armstrong.*

Huncoat Station. 14th May 1952. This 1952 view towards Accrington shows the somewhat shabby blackened red brick buildings on the Up platform. The grime was no doubt due to the heavy industrial presence around Huncoat although the rather austere design of the station buildings, somewhat unusual by L. & Y. standards, probably did not help. Gas lighting would survive well into the next decade and it would also be some time before British Railways maroon enamel signs made an appearance. Other features which identified its ancestry included the substantial platform copings with their bull nosed profile and the lattice footbridge, although not complete, with overhead bracing, a traditional company feature. *G. Biddle.*

Huncoat Station (2). As we stand in the brick loading sidings near to the tall Huncoat Crossing signalbox a passing excursion from Bradford 1X18 prevents us from seeing the level crossing and the loop of the colliery sidings. *Dave Dyson.*

Huncoat station.

Beyond the power station the line would lead into a cutting with a couple of overbridges. This cutting would prevent us seeing much of the colliery at Huncoat, which was situated to the right side of the railway on the run into Huncoat station. Only the winding gear and engine house etc. were visible at this stage. As we passed under the second of the two bridges, before us lay the platforms of Huncoat and over to the right behind the Down platform were the colliery exchange sidings which were always full of traffic, be it coal from the pit or coke from Altham coke works. An extended head shunt from these sidings, was positioned near to the level crossing gates. Additional usage of the sidings was made by the numerous local brick firms. During the 50's, coal coke and brick traffic was constantly being shunted in and out of the sidings behind Huncoat's station platforms. The whole area around Huncoat was full of industry, with coal mines, quarries and brick works filling the area across to Altham and Clayton le Moors. Huncoat colliery still employed as many as 550 miners well into the 1960's with two out of the three coal faces remaining in use. One of these faces was connected through to Calder Colliery near Simonstone, which was some miles away. Mining at Huncoat would not cease until 1968, by which time the workforce had been drastically reduced. The name Dicky Pit is probably more well remembered than Huncoat Colliery despite the fact that it closed many years earlier. Dicky Pit, also called Hargreaves colliery, had the official name of "The Moorfields Colliery and Chemical Works, Altham". Mine workings there would cease in 1949, but the coking plant would remain in use for a number of years after that. A mineral railway edged out across the valley from Huncoat towards Clayton le Moors and Dicky Pit and it was along this mineral branch line that the coal and coke traffic was transferred to the main line. The large coke ovens at the Altham works would produce many thousands of tons of coke over the years. Further over the valley in the Accrington direction two large quarries at Whinney Hill and Enfield provided the raw materials for the brickworks in the area such as the " NORI" and "RED - AC" plants (Huncoat Brick and Tile Co.) Brick loading sites included the sidings situated behind the tall level crossing signal box (Huncoat station cabin), but the main storage point for the brick traffic was nearer to Accrington. Huncoat station itself was hardly ever called at in the 1950s by the excursions from Colne, but the brief glimpses we did get revealed a tidy if shabby looking place whose red brick buildings had suffered badly from the smoke of the industrial surroundings, again an unusual feature on the platforms were a number of large black iron flower tubs with lions heads upon them. How they came to be at Huncoat is a mystery. A wide level crossing sat at the west end of the station and the tall Huncoat station signal box stood guard next to the up side of the line. The next signal box was to be found at the bottom of the loops which ran down from Huncoat towards Accrington. This box was known simply as Accrington Brick and situated behind the signal box were a number of brick storage sidings and a branch line which curved away past the nearby cricket ground towards the "Nori" and "Enfield" brickworks. From the high position on the banking at Accrington Brick signal box we were quickly plunged into a rock cutting as the line dropped steadily down towards Accrington. This descent down the rock cutting was brief, and suddenly the area of green belt and industry was transformed into a broad vista of suburbia. Dropping down past the Borough Laundry, the elevated approach to Accrington gave us a fine view right across the valley in which the town was situated. From the valley base right up to the distant hills on the far side, the scene was one of rows of terraced houses together with wide array of mill chimneys. The descent to Accrington was swift and the sudden heavy braking on the approach to the twisting viaduct almost had us tumbling onto the seats opposite. As we crept slowly over the viaduct at 10 mph, looking over to our right it was possible to see the works of the famous Accrington firm of Messrs. Entwistle and Kenyon, better known as Ewbank, due to the world famous carpet sweeper that they produced. Accrington was famous for a number of things, the ubiquitous Ewbank carpet sweeper being undoubtably the towns biggest claim to fame but Accrington is also remembered as the birthplace of George Formby's wife, Beryl Ingham, and as football fans will recall, the town had a very popular football club in the shape of Accrington Stanley, whose home matches were played upon a sloping pitch. Such was the popularity of the famed Ewbank carpet sweeper, that few homes in the 1950s would be without one. When we think of those who would have used the various excursions to the seaside, it becomes quite clear that a fair number of the 1000 or so workers at the Ewbank works would have patronised the railways at the local holidays. The firm had a long association with the railway at Accrington and carpet sweepers and small washing and drying machines would leave the town's station for all parts of the country. The firm branched into small domestic washing machines and handy spin dryers in the 1950s and also did a steady trade in the tubular kitchen furniture that was so popular in that era. Entwistle and Kenyon became part of the Prestige kitchenware group in 1960 and this really was the beginning of the end for the Ewbank plant. The famous carpet sweeper first saw the light of day in 1889 and it would be a bestseller for a great many years. However, changing trends and fitted carpets demanded something more suitable and by the 1950s, Entwistle and Kenyon found themselves facing stiff competition from the modern electric vacuum cleaners. The Ewbank market was quickly eroded in the 1960s with manual carpet sweepers quickly becoming a thing of the past.

Huncoat Brick No.**90407** again of Wakefield clatters past the former sidings at Huncoat Brick signalbox. Here a number of storage sidings and a tight curved branch line served the nearby brick works in the Huncoat area. *Noel Coates.*

Entwistle and Kenyon Ltd. Mention the above name to someone and it will mean little. Say Ewbank and it would be a very different story. The famous carpet sweeper was made in Accrington at a factory not too far from the town's high railway viaduct. In the 1950s some 1000 workers still produced a variety of items at the works but still the most famous was the ubiquitous Ewbank ......! Some of those named in the photograph are as follows: 1) N. Walkden, 2) J. Nuttall and T. Yates, 3) Joe Casson, 4) M. Bond, 5) I. Wills, 6) D. Heywood, 7) D. Howlker, 8) R. Doherty.

(courtesy Accrington Library, Lancashire C. Libraries.).

High Above the Rooftops. The long twisting viaduct at Accrington stood high above the town, affording unique views of typical mill town Lancashire, and a busy place it really was in the 1950s. In the back ground the railway climbed up to Huncoat past the Borough Laundry. Huncoat power station is on the skyline.

Eddie Bobrowski.

Accrington Station. The way we knew it in the 1950s, the Bury Manchester route to the left (platforms 2 and 3), the Blackburn line is to the right (platform 5), in No.6 platform is a Preston - York special C 870 with No.**45574** *India* on Whit Monday 18th May 1959.
Dave Dyson.

Accrington station.

The station was situated close to the west end of the viaduct and looking down upon the town at this point we had a fine view of the main shopping area, which was over to the left, the solid stone structures of the town hall and market visible some distance away. The approach to the station was very cautious and the coach wheels protested loudly as they took the severe right hand curve into the station itself. Our compartment shook as the bogie beneath us wrenched its way round the tight curve and you somehow got the impression that had the speed exceeded the 10mph greatly, then we would have come to earth with a bump. Looking out of the left side of the compartment, our first glimpse of the station was a view of the old East Lancashire Railway buildings which stood close to the edge of the viaduct. These buildings sat upon a wide low section of flagged platform, which curved to the left away from the direction in which we were travelling. This old section of platform continued at a low level for some distance along what was the main Manchester platform (No.2) and where the East Lancs. buildings gave way to more modern structures, the platform rose up to normal platform height. This number two platform was extensively used for the handling of parcels traffic and the parcels offices were situated close by. Mountains of mail and piles of parcels were to be seen on the busy platform awaiting loading etc. A wide range of items either made or stored locally would be despatched from this point and worthy of mention here are the products of Messrs. Entwistle and Kenyon (Ewbank) and the Dept. of Health, who had storage mills in the Oswaldtwistle area containing items of help to the handicapped and, as a result, many hundreds of wheel chairs passed through the Accrington parcel offices. Parcel trains from Colne etc. would draw into platform two to off-load and load mail, after which they would reverse back onto the viaduct before proceeding on their way to Preston. Likewise, parcels workings from Preston would draw through the station and out onto the viaduct before reversing into number two platform to sort the mail; incidentally the colour lights and stencil indicators in use at the Accrington East signalbox to control these moves would be amongst the first of their type in our area. Further along the Manchester platform, the bay platform No.1 was to be found tucked away to the left and a number of sidings formed a small yard next to this. Road access to here was provided from the corner of the station yard in Eagle street. The awesome 1 in 38 of Baxenden bank would commence at the end of these Manchester bound platforms and a sand drag was provided on the down line right up to the station approaches at Ormerod Street bridge. A banking engine was provided 22 hours a day for the incline and usually in the late 1940s and 50s you'd see an Austerity 2-8-0 simmering in the siding adjacent to Eagle Street, waiting to push a train up the bank. The lines surrounding the station formed a wide triangle, and excursion traffic from such places as Radcliffe seemed to be routed each year via Bury and Ramsbottom to Accrington. Possibly the reason why these Radcliffe holiday specials took this round about route through Eas

Town Holiday 'Runabout Tickets'

SECOND 30/- CLASS

AVAILABLE FOR SIX DAYS BY ANY TRAIN

SUNDAY to FRIDAY, 16th to 21st JULY
or 23rd to 28th JULY

These Tickets are issued from Stations and Agencies and allow
UNRESTRICTED TRAVEL between

ACCRINGTON, CHURCH and OSWALDTWISTLE,
HELMSHORE, HUNCOAT and HAPTON

and Southport, Blackpool, Fleetwood, Preston, Lancaster, Morecambe, Windermere Town, Arnside, Grange, Barrow and Millom. Also available between Ulverston and Lakeside and including Sailings on Lake Windermere by B.R. Steamers between all Piers
WITHOUT EXTRA CHARGE
NOT AVAILABLE BY SPECIAL DIESEL EXCURSIONS

Enquire for details of "Runabout" Tickets in North Wales, The English Lakes and West Cumberland

		A
		Halifax to Southport
		C 542
		am
Hebden Bridge	dep	..
Hall Royd Jn.		..
TODMORDEN		..
Walsden		..
Littleborough		..
Smithy Bridge		..
ROCHDALE		..
Portsmouth		Also conveys passengers to Rose Grove for C820 Football Halfex Accrington to Leeds City South
Copy Pit		
Burnley M.Rd.		
Snaygill		
SKIPTON	arr	
	dep	
Skipton North Jn.	arr	
	dep	
Earby		
Barnoldswick		
Foulridge		
COLNE	arr	..
	dep	11 55
Nelson		12 0
Brierfield		12 4
BURNLEY CEN.		12 10
Burnley Barracks		12 13
Rose Grove East	arr	..
	dep	..
Rose Grove		12 18
Padiham		..
Hapton		..
Huncoat		..
ACCRINGTON		12c29
Accrington South Jn.		..
Church		12 33
Rishton		12 39
BLACKBURN	arr	12 46
	dep	12 48
Mill Hill		12 52
Cherry Tree		..
Pleasington		..
Hoghton		..
Bamber Bridge		1 3
Todd Lane Jn.		1 5
Lostock Hall Jn.		..
Whitehouse South Jn.		1 .7

Accrington North. 30:08:58. Just before 12/30 at dinnertime on Saturday 30th August 1958, on what was to be a glorious summers day, hot and humid, Lower Darwen B.R. Class 4 No.**76081** on loan to Rose Grove depot, works C542, the 11.55am Colne to Blackpool Central "Halfex". This train also conveyed football fans from Colne to Rose Grove in order that they could catch C820 - an Accrington to Leeds City South special, taking fans of Accrington Stanley to Leeds for an away match. C542 is seen coming off the viaduct at Accrington and the loco is about to enter Platform 5. The lines curving away to the right are those for the steep 1 in 38 Baxenden Bank. *Dave Dyson.*

Lancashire, would be that it kept them away from the busy lines around the Bolton and Lostock areas. Having reached the foot of Baxenden bank these specials would travel round the angle from Ormerod street on the south side of Accrington to Accrington West signal box passing en-route the goods warehouses situated on the angle. These trains would then head off towards Preston and the Fylde coast. Our excursion trips through Accrington always took us via Platform 5 and as we curved away from the Manchester route, the train would pass under the red and cream painted footbridge which connected all the various platforms. This footbridge had a water supply running along it and engines could replenish their water tanks whilst standing in the station, providing that is if the driver stopped his loco. in the right place. The rather elaborate structure of the footbridge was steel panelled instead of being of the lattice type and it was complete with glazing and an overall roof. It was quite usual to draw well down the platform at Accrington. Drawing up with these excursion was also the order of the day as this helped to fill the empty compartments at the rear and this latter sequence would see us standing close to the very ornate water column which was located at the West Junction of the triangle. While all this was going on, dad would be by the carriage door his large frame filling the window, still with pad and pen in hand ready for jotting down any engines that may come into view. He'd draw heavily on the Player's cigarette hanging from his mouth, the compartment was stuffy and the warm summer sun hitting the compartment windows made us feel as if we were in a greenhouse. Beads of perspiration dotted dad's forehead as he anxiously waited to note the number of the clanking Austerity 2-8-0 which was making its way round the angle past the goods sheds. Shouts of "mind the doors" and the sound of whistles in the distance behind indicated to us that we'd soon be under way again, but not before we give a brief mention to the buildings on No.5 platform. These structures, as with those over on No.6 platform, were of wood construction and were painted in red and cream. The red was applied to the lower part of the walls and the doors, the main area of the walls and the awning was in cream. The platform decking on Nos. 5 & 6 were made of wood and these were rebuilt in the late 1950s with concrete sections, as was the cattle dock to the rear of Platform 6, subsidence of the platforms having affected Accrington for a great many years. Platform 4, the west bay, was also refurbished along with the other platforms using concrete sections. Ticket offices were situated on Platforms 2 and 6 respectively and refreshment rooms were located on the main platforms at one time. In the triangle of the station, once stood the original East Lancs. Rly. engine sheds and even in the 1950s, there was still some sort of tank house within that area. Close by this old stone tank house was a more modern water tower, mounted upon a tall steel frame which towered above the station buildings. Accrington station to us in the 1950s seemed a very busy place and despite the fact that our two holiday periods were at different times, there would always be an healthy number of passengers waiting to join our seaside specials on the few occasions when we did travel that way.

Holiday Crowd. The wooden decking of Accrington's No.5 platform is crowded as yet another seaside special enters the platform. No.**42845** was an "extra" in the Arthur Askey film "The Love Match". It was seen in the film resting on Bolton shed in 1954. *Dave Dyson*

ACCRINGTON

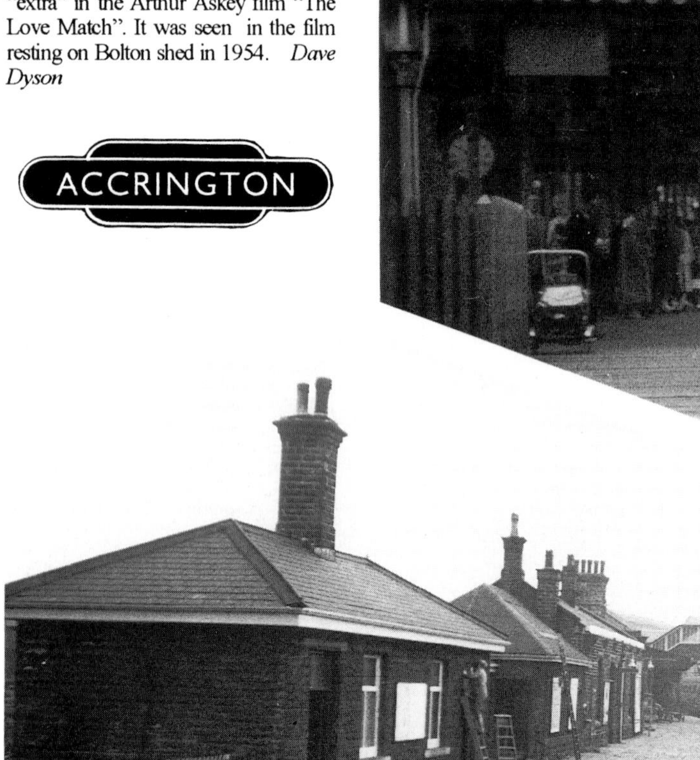

The E.L. Buildings (1). Seen from the train the original low level platform and East Lancs. Railway buildings always seemed well looked after even in the 1950s and 60s, the low platform despite having little use was kept free of weeds etc. (July 1958). *G.H. Platt*

BELLE VUE 5/-

Reduced Admission tickets to the Gardens

Adults 1/6, Children 9d extra obtainable at time of booking rail tickets

TUESDAY and THURSDAY 18th and 20th JULY

Accrington ...... dep. 12.50 p.m.
Church & O .... dep. 12.55 p.m.
Belle Vue .... ret. 8.25 p.m.

THURSDAY, 27th JULY

Accrington ...... dep. 12.25 p.m.
Church & O. .... 12.28 p.m.
Belle Vue .... ret. 8.08 p.m.

ALTON TOWERS 11/3

SUNDAY, 23rd JULY

Accrington . dep. 9.50 a.m.
Church & O. dep. 9.54 a.m.
Alton Towers ret. 6.55 p.m.

The E.L. Buildings (2). A well framed view, the sort of scene we saw returning at night, this was Accrington just as we knew it in the 50s; clean tidy and well looked after. Again note the low platform and the way the slope leads down to the barrow crossing. Above, mounted to the underside of the footbridge, was the water column. *G.H.Platt.*

"Getting to Grips". No.**45679** *Armada* takes Accrington South curve with a return excursion C549 to Radcliffe in 1959. You can almost hear the "Woof woof" of the exhaust as, with sanders hard on, the driver coaxes his engine round the tight curve, ahead of him the gruelling 1 in 38 of Baxenden bank. *Dave Dyson.*

"With the Guard" Having dashed at the last minute to catch a Largs special in 1960, Margaret (Betty) Payne, future wife of Dave Dyson, had to make do with the brakevan. Whilst Margaret wasn't amused, Dave didn't mind. *Dave Dyson (courtesy of Betty).*

Holiday Bookings. Over to the right we see the main booking hall area, access was from Eagle Street and passengers bound for Blackpool etc. would have to walk over the footbridge to platform 5. The busy parcels office was also on the Eagle Street side. The interior of the booking office, as we can see in the picture below, was very similar to many others to be seen along the East Lancs. line. Extra staff would be drafted in to cope with the added demand for tickets at the holidays. The sort of destinations available at the holidays and the fare scales are seen to the lower right with the cheap day ticket to Blackpool being a mere 5/9d. In the two pictures on the lower page we have a view of platform No.2 and the parcels handling area. and at the bottom of the page is the view from No.2 looking over towards platforms 5 and 6, which were the main Blackburn and Colne platforms respectively. *British Railways.*

CHESTER 10/6; PRESTATYN 15/-. RHYL 15/6; ABERGELE 16/6 COLWYN BAY 18/-; LLANDUDNO Junct. 19/-; LLANDUDNO 19/-

TUESDAY and THURSDAY 18th and 20th JULY

Accrington ...... dep. 9.05 a.m.
Church & O. .... dep. 9.09 a.m.

TUESDAY, 25th JULY

Accrington ...... dep. 9.05 a.m.
Church & O. .... dep. 9.09 a.m.

LIVERPOOL 9/9

WITH BOOKINGS TO.

NEW BRIGHTON

(via Ferry 12/1, or Mersey Line 11/-)

HOYLAKE 12/-
WEST KIRBY 12/3

(via Mersey Line)

MONDAY, 17th JULY

Accrington ...... dep. 9.05 a.m.
Church & O. .... dep. 9.09 a.m.
Liverpool Ex. .... ret. 7.05 p.m.

BLACKPOOL 5/9

SUNDAY, 16th JULY

Accrington ...... dep. 8.50 a.m.
Church & O. .... dep. 8.54 a.m.
Blackpool Cent .. ret. 6.50 p.m.

MON. to WED. 17th to 19th JULY

Accrington ...... dep. 8.40 a.m.
Church & O. .... dep. 8.44 a.m.
Blackpool Cent. .. ret. 7.00 p.m.

MON TUES and WED 24th, 25th and 26th JULY

Accrington ...... dep. 9.30 a.m.
Church & O. .... dep 9.34 a.m.
Blackpool Cent. .. ret. 6.35 p.m.

SOUTHPORT

MON to WED, 17th to 19th JULY and MON and TUES 24th and 25th JULY

Accrington .. dep 9.48 a.m. 7/3
Church & O .. dep. 9.50 a.m. 7/0

MORECAMBE 7/6

TUESDAY and THURSDAY 18th and 20th JULY

Accrington ...... dep. 10.20 a.m.
Church & O. .... dep. 10.24 a.m.
Morecambe E. Rd ret. 6.30 p.m.

COMBINED RAIL AND STEAMER TOUR TO

KYLES OF BUTE 48/-

(Buffet Car Train)

By Rail to Largs allowing approx 1½ hours stay, then steamer cruise to Rothesay via the Cumbraes, Garroch Head and the Kyles of Bute Approx 2 hours stay allowed at Rothesay before re-embarking for Largs and return rail journey

MONDAY, 24th JULY

Accrington . dep. 6.17 a.m.
Church & O dep. 6.21 a.m.
Largs ...... ret. 7.45 p.m

Packed Lunches at 5/- each will be provided on the outward journey if booked in advance prior to 10.00 a.m. Friday, 21st July.

Accommodation strictly limited and bookings will close when all seats have been booked.

Book in Advance

HOLIDAY RECORDS ALL THE WAY

THEY can't wait to get out of Accrington fast enough — with a quarter of a million pounds in their holiday pockets!

Road and travel agencies report holiday records, records—all the way.

By now Accrington people are "rarin' to go" and the gloomy weather at home has made them all the keener.

With more in their pockets following a year of full employment, more people than ever are going away this year for the full fortnight.

Altham's Travel Agency, say that advanced rail bookings in June show a 17 per cent increase on last year, while the May bookings were 50 per cent up on the year before.

The increase in rail bookings has surprised Althams. Said Mr Sutcliffe, the local manager, "All the allocations of rail tickets have been exceeded, and we have had to apply to British Railways, Manchester, for increases particularly for the Isle of Man and the South Coast and West of England."

Mr Sutcliffe pointed out that many of the bookings are from Church and Oswaldtwistle, and the impression given out at Church Station early this week of a slump in bookings from Church and Oswaldtwistle is contradicted in Altham's experience.

Bookings to holiday camps are down and rail bookings to Filey are fewer.

The explanation seems to be that people who took camp holidays last year are going on the Continent this time.

Blackpool Central 16.5.53. Platform 11 at Blackpool's Central station is the scene in the top picture on this page. No.**45068** stands at the buffer stops, having just arrived with one of the 13 special trains carrying Howard and Bullough's workers and their relatives on the centenary outing in May 1953. Over 7000 people were transported in the 13 trains. The one that didn't go was manned by driver Herbert Dobson and fireman Neil Godwin who spent the whole of their shift on the old "Crab" loco. sat in the sidings at Accrington. *Frank Watson.*

Howard and Bullough Ltd.,

It would not be possible to pass Accrington station or indeed Accrington as a whole without seeing the huge "Globe" works of textile machinery giants Howard and Bullough. The various mills which comprised the firm stood out across the town from whichever angle you care to mention. The main façade on Scaitcliff Street towered above the railway station and large neon letters sat on the roof proclaiming the company's name. The firm started in the 1850s and it would expand over the years opening up foundries and machine shops making spinning and weaving preparation equipment. By the mid 1920s, they would be the town's biggest employer and by the time the Second World War broke out the company included other engineering firms such as Platts, the workforce of some 6000 providing shells, smoke bombs, gun carriages and bomber fuselages for the war effort. May 16th 1953 saw the firm celebrate its centenary by taking its workers for a day trip to Blackpool, all expenses paid. A total of £10,000 was spent hiring 14 special trains to take the workers and their families to the coast. Actually, 13 of the trains ran and one stayed spare at Accrington. It was very much a one off event, never to be seen again on the railway at Accrington. Driver Jim Scott and fireman Tom Whelan worked the first excursion into Blackpool and received Carnation button holes from the Mayor and Mayoress of Blackpool upon arrival at the town's Central station. More than 7000 workers and their relatives took advantage of this special outing. The spare excursion train, which Howard and Bullough did not require, was manned by fireman Neil Godwin and driver Herbert Dobson. Apparently they spent the whole of their eight hour shift sat in the cab of their Crab loco. in the carriage sheds without turning a wheel. Herbert, incidentally suffered badly with his feet and therefore wore pumps rather than boots or clogs and due to crouching down by the engines a lot, both his toes and the pumps tended to curl up at the ends and as a result Herbert was known as being " FULL OF EASTERN PROMISE"... ! On a more sombre note, Howard and Bullough, in keeping with many large manufacturing industries connected with the cotton industry, began to decline seriously in the late 1950s and the famous "Globe" works, the first in the area to use electric lighting, would close some thirty years after those centenary specials ran to Blackpool.

(Above and right) **"Jocko's"** This was the term often used for the shunt engines and two main types seemed to frequent Accrington. The old "Lanky" A Class tank like the one above right (No.**51497**) and the other, a standard Fowler shunter, however one other memorable tanky was No.**47201**, which as we see here on the right appears to be almost ex-works as it shunts tar tanks destined for Metcalfes at Church and Oswaldtwistle. In the picture (above)of No.**51497**, the railwaymen are Herman Rose (shunter), Frank Sagar (driver), Jacky Wright (shunter), W Mould (fireman) and W Whitehouse (guard). *Dave Dyson and Len Wesson.*

Accrington West to Aspen Colliery.

The west end of Accrington could prove quite busy, with light engines moving to and from the shed together with goods and passenger shunters pottering about; the scene really was hectic at times. The Accrington West signalman would control the easterly approaches to the shed and it was at this end of the shed area that the carriage shed stood. It covered six roads and in later years concrete bases were laid along the shed roads for easy cleaning of diesel spillage from the new diesel railcars. The roof of the shed had also been updated around the mid 1950s, again in readiness for the diesel era. By 1960 much of the maroon coaching stock we had grown accustomed to seeing at Accrington had given way to the shiny green painted railcars. These were built by the Cravens Company at Sheffield, a firm more normally associated with the construction of buses, which is possibly why the windows of the new units vibrated so much ...! Soon these modern diesel units would monopolise the carriage shed area. Coaching stock was still to be found in some quantity in the 1960s and it was this stock which prevented us as a rule from getting a decent glimpse of the shed itself. March 1961 would see the last of the steamers move away to Rose Grove and Lostock Hall and with them would go a number of shed staff including drivers and firemen who wished to remain on steam. Motive power for the shunt turns was then provided by Rose Grove and in fact one of their diagrams was known as the Accrington carriage shunt. Often in the summer this turn of duty would see them taking an excursion to Blackpool rather than shunting the sidings. As we passed the carriage sidings and the shed you were nearly always unable to get a clear view of the coal stage and ash pit because of the coaching stock and goods wagons in the exchange sidings near to Church East and it wasn't until we reached the Church end that a clear look across to the shed roads was possible and again this glimpse was only brief giving little time to catch the numbers of engines on shed. Sometimes we'd be lucky and dad would shout "here thy are, 45068 42294" and there near the turntable we'd be treated to a fleeting glance of the two steam engines. The turntable at Accrington shed would remain in use long after the steam engines left as a means of turning the diesel railcars as and when required.

Goods facilities at Accrington.

On the South to West curve of the Accrington triangle the busy goods depot was situated. The warehouses and travelling crane system there handled all manner of goods, including machinery from the nearby plant of Howard and Bullough Ltd., many of their products being bound for the docks for shipment abroad. Tar wagons would arrive at the Accrington goods depot and they would then be "tripped down" to Church and "Ossie" for Metcalfes the tar distillers. Whilst the goods depot tended to deal with general goods items, there were one or two coal yards including the large one adjacent to the down goods exchange sidings to be seen on the run down to Church and Oswaldtwistle.

"**Fare - Do's**"...! Rose Grove driver Winston Hartley (seen right) had a brother who was in a bit of a band in the 1960s and he needed a new organ. Winston arranged to meet him down Accrington after work to get the organ, after which they'd planned to bring it back on the train. As they struggled to hoist it into the brakevan of a DMU, round came the guard, Wilf Bridge (seen left). He shouted "I HOPE YOU'VE PAID FOR THAT .....! (meaning freight carraige for the organ). Winston replied using typical Lancashire humour " NOOW, WI ' GORRIT ONT H. P. ....!

Eric Laycock / Raymond Short.

Accrington No.6 Platform. As we sat in our non-corridor compartment in No.5 platform we had chance to look across at the somewhat shabby woodwork over on No.6, the platform for Colne. The lower part of the buildings had become a faded red whilst the top portion had at one time been cream, but was now a shade of dirty yellow and rust brown. *British Railways.*

Accrington Holidays 1960. Looking west towards the diesel running shed, (in the Church and Oswaldtwistle direction), this was the view from the end of Accrington's No.5 platform. Borrowed Ivatt class 4 (Doodlebug) No.**43033** is the train engine, just out of Horwich works, all stiff and smelling of fresh paint no doubt. Accrington driver Johnny Kearns is at the regulator as this "Halfex" to Blackpool gets under way on Sunday the 17th July 1960. The train code was C550.
Dave Dyson

The New Order. Just beyond Accrington's West Junction was the diesel running shed, formerly the main carriage servicing shed. The DMU's had by 1960/61 virtually taken over the sheds. The line to the extreme left leads round to the old steam shed and coaling plant etc. On the right is the main line down to Church.
Courtesy of Frank Watson.

Accrington Motive Power Depot.

Long before the arrival of the diesels in 1960 the shed was a very important depot with regard to the local passenger services of East Lancashire. By far the largest amount of the depots work revolved around these many local passenger jobs. These services included the following routes, Skipton - Colne - Blackpool, Midge Hall and Liverpool Exchange, Todmorden and Wakefield, as well as the locals to Manchester via Baxenden and Bury. A wide range of routes were covered, relying on some good road knowledge on the part of the crews. Many of those regularly driving were still only "passed" men with little hope of getting "Booked" so long as they stayed at the shed, as always it really was a case of "deadman's shoes", waiting for a driver to come off the job for one reason or another. The motive power used in the fifties on these passenger workings was in the main, Stanier Class 4 tanks and also the later Fairburn variety, which were not as popular due to their rougher riding qualities, everything seeming to vibrate and rattle far more than the Stanier types. Black 5 4-6-0's had by the late 1950s taken over from the old Midland Compounds and Class 2 4-4-0's on these passenger diagrams. Accrington's Crab 2-6-0's would also have moved away to Rose Grove and Lower Darwen. Engines which readily spring to mind at Accrington in the latter part of the fifties are No.42110, (probably the last local engine to retain the wording British Railways in full on the tank sides), Nos.42153, 42294, 42295, 42643, 44689, 44692 and 45068. Diesel railcars had been a familiar sight at Accrington from as early as 1956 when the Bury sets used on the Bacup services took part in crew training sessions in the area. Accrington's own railcars- which were forever known as "Accrington sets"- came in two stages for the dieselisation of the Skipton - Colne - Blackpool and the Colne - Manchester services between January 1960 and March of 1961. The later Cravens' sets with the "Torque"converter gearboxes were easily distinguished from the earlier types fitted with the standard gear change by their large headcode boxes on the roof. With the arrival of the railcars the last few Fairburn tanks and Black 5's left the shed for pastures new. On the goods side of things coal trains, fitted freights and shunt and trip work was undertaken at Accrington. Trip working included shunting the busy Huncoat sidings of coal, coke and bricks, tripping up to Blythes siding for the scrap dock and tank roads, also Metcalfes tar distillers. These jobs would include going up to Rishton, which had considerable coal traffic in the 1950s. Local shunt jobs involved the warehouse shunt by the station and the two exchange yards down by Church East, known as the Up and Down Sidings. Shunting the Up Exchange Yard was unusual as normally headshunts at yards climbed up-hill making it easy to hook wagons off and let them roll into the various roads. However at Accrington, shunting was done the opposite way round and engines would draw a string of wagons out of one of the sidings down to the headshunt, then it was a case of "get at em" and the regulator would be flung right over in full forward gear and the little "A" class tank locomotive would charge up-hill to the sidings. This type of shunting was twice as demanding on both men and machinery. Longer haul goods workings would see the Accrington men working to and from Manchester on the "Mostons" and over to Wigan's Bamfurlong Sidings on the coal jobs. With regard to the shed itself, the coaling plant was of the modern concrete hopper type and the ash plant had been updated at a similar time, (thought to be around 1934 - 35 period). From the ashpit the locos. would need to run down towards Church East to use the turntable which was situated down the side of the shed. Some of the shed link drivers had acquired the art of dropping engines down off the ash pit with little steam in them and Tommy Rodd was one of these. By timing it just right and using the tender handbrake, he could get an engine to come gently to a stand on the "table", but as you can imagine, things didn't always go to plan and now and again the odd steamer would career across the turntable, mount the banking and drop into someone's back yard down in Lonsdale Street. It was just lucky on a few occasions that the turntable was facing the right way, otherwise the engine coming rumbling down by the shed corner would have dropped into the turntable well. Then as always the services of the shed gang and fitters together with the "Chipperfields" (nickname for the steam crane) would be required. The shed buildings provided covered accommodation over 6 of the 8 shed roads. Number 7 and 8 roads sat between the shed and the goods warehouse close by Charter street. Howard and Bullough would bring machinery, crated and destined for foreign parts, to this goods loading point ready for shipping to the docks. The sidings leading to the warehouse had also dealt with coal traffic at some time for the Co-op. Shed roads 7 and 8 had at one time been covered, back in the days of the old northlight roofing and when the shed roof was reconstructed these two roads were omitted. The shape of the northlight roof could be seen in the areas on the goods shed wall where the lead flashing had kept the brickwork clean from the surrounding blackening elements. Shed roads 7 and 8, covered or not, still provided good protection from the elements, especially in winter, and it was here that locomotives were usually stored. Some engines such as the old Midland Compounds and Class 2's would end their days alongside the side of the shed here. They were not well liked and would only come out of store in the summer months when all else failed. By the mid 1950s "better tackle" had arrived in the shape of Black 5's and B.R. Standard locos. and the old Midland engines spent more and more time in store. British Railways Standard Class 4 4-6-0's arrived in the winter of 1953/54, numbers 75045-49 coming brand new. They proved very popular, having excellent injectors, rocking fire grates and hopper ashpan plus protection from the elements; you bet they were popular! In their short stay at Accrington they would be seen on all manner of passenger work, even the seaside specials. All too soon these fine little engines moved away to Bank Hall, to be replaced by Stanier and Fairburn tanks. The shed compliment would be made up of three main links which covered the many passenger workings and the various freight turns. There would also be the pilot jobs (shunt engine drivers) and shed links, those men brought off the main line for one reason or another, around 125 sets of men in all. If you add to that the shed labourers on the ashpits etc. and the fitting staff, it becomes clear that together with the Carriage and Wagon fitters, cleaners and other carriage shed staff, that there was quite a workforce in the Accrington shed area.

Behind the Sheds 25.8.55. Tucked away behind the carriage sheds at Accrington was this old L and Y Rly. Barton Wright tank engine in use as a steam heating boiler. The locomotive must have never turned a wheel in years. It was just like the two we always saw next to platform 7 at Blackpool Central. *Brian E Morrison*

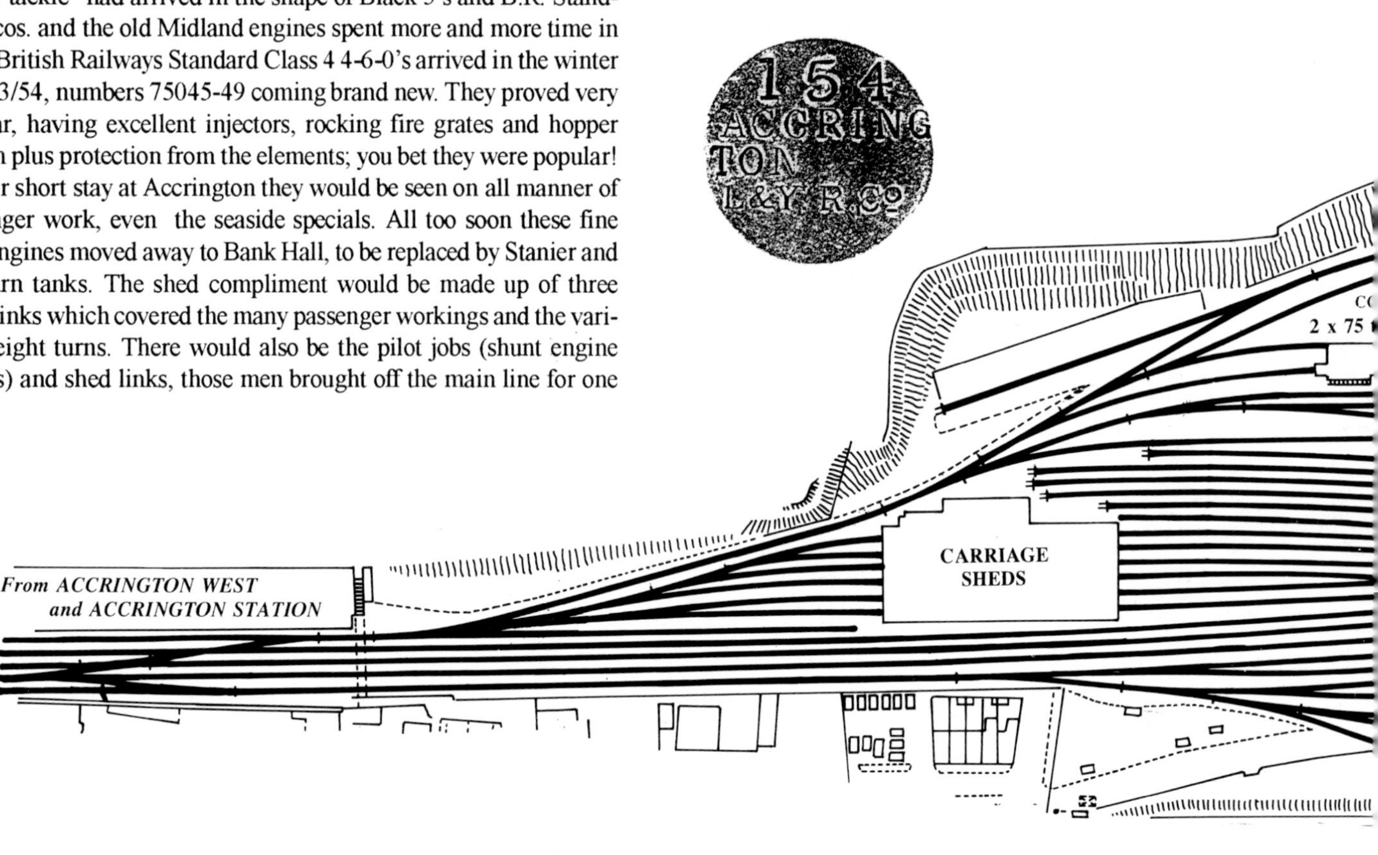

One of the Best. No**42643** rests on Accrington shed on Thursday 25th August 1955. In conversation, a number of Accrington men mentioned this loco., in particular saying,"2643, aye she were a gud'n, one ert best"! The riding qualities of these Stanier tanks was far superior to the later Fairburn types. It is hard to imagine looking at her that within 5 years she would be redundant as the DMU's came in.

Brian E Morrison.

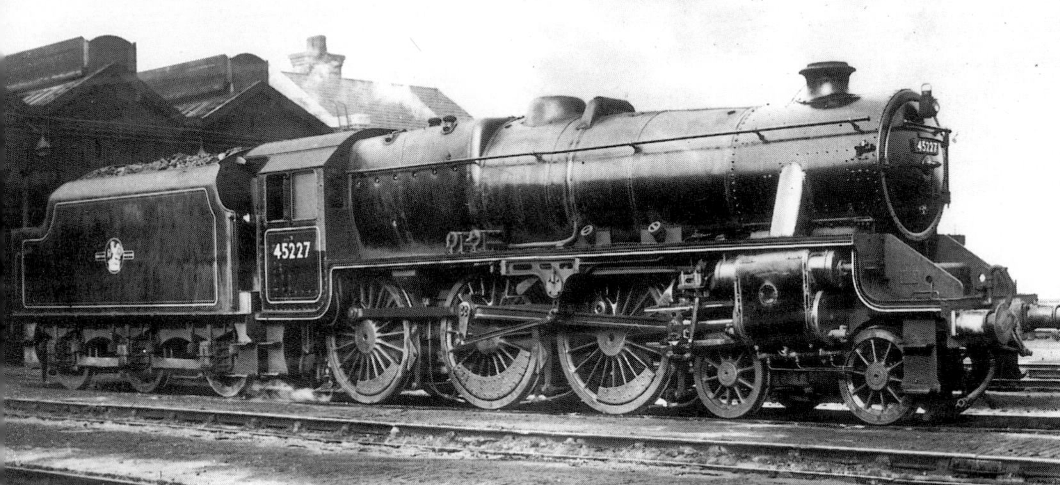

On Shed. Two more views of the early 50s at Accrington shed, are seen below, No.**45227** looks a picture "all Bulled up" as it sits on the shed road, and (above) we see a young Frank Watson as a cleaner complete with new uniform in 1951 (seen in the cab of No.**45396**).

Courtesy of Frank Watson.

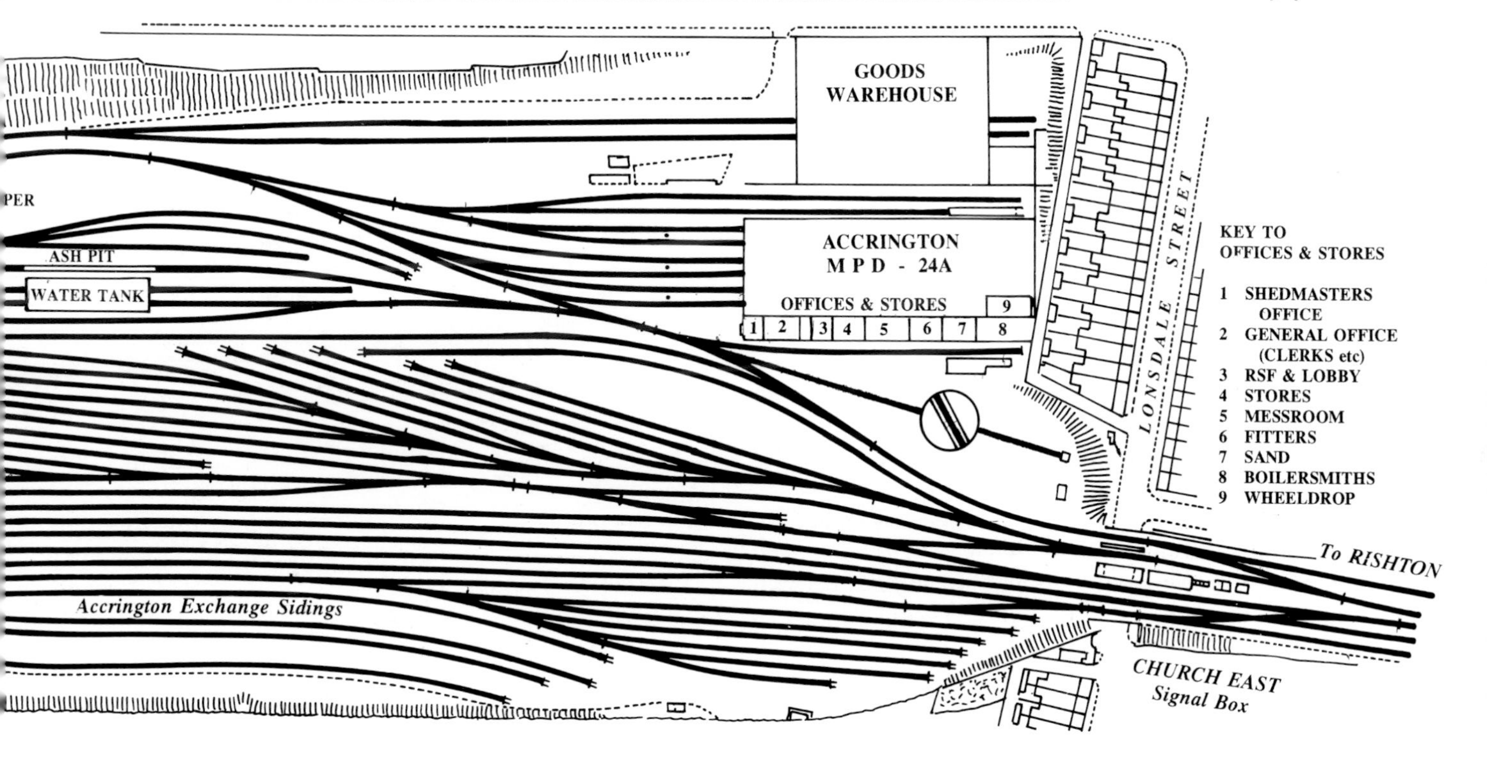

Summer workings from Accrington,

(memories of the late 1940s and early 50s).

Working the many summer extras to the Lancashire coast became a regular performance for young Accrington firemen such as Neil Godwin and Ray Thorpe. Both Neil and Ray have happy memories of the 1950s on those excursion workings. Usually these workings were extra days to the normal working week and getting paid on your "Rest Day" to work to Blackpool couldn't be bad !. Ray's regular mate driver Charlie Terry had been a "Midland" man originating at Manningham depot at Bradford and later moved to Lancaster Green Ayre before transferring to Accrington. He had a wide route knowledge and he and Ray would occasionally work over the Ilkley line to Guiseley and round to Bradford's Forster Square station. Charlie was also familiar with the line from Skipton across to Carnforth and of course the line to Green Ayre from Wennington. Charlie, when working an excursion to Morecambe via Preston, would travel the distance between Preston and Lancaster in 19 minutes - expresses in modern times are allowed 23 minutes for the same run. He'd dash through Lancaster Castle flat out and head out across the Lune bridge, and approaching Morecambe South Junction, he'd "slap" the brake on, sliding round the curve towards Bare Lane. Off would come the brake and Charlie would open up again to hoist the train through Bare Lane station, en-route to Morecambe's Euston Road station a short distance away. This method of "slapping the brake on" and then blowing it off again soon after may seem a bit dramatic and somewhat of an erratic way to drive, but on the contrary, this was the art of working these excursion trains to the best effect. Great skill and enginemanship together with good road knowledge was required in order to drive in this manner. The Enfield Manufacturing Co. were amongst the regular firms outings in the fifties to use the railway, bringing with them of course their own supply of beer, and Ray chuckles as he recalls how a wooden crate of beer bottles would often be chucked onto the engine footplate "for the lads".

Blackpool was a favourite for the day trips out and on one occasion when Ray and his mate for the day, driver Len Dickey, (Dickinson) were returning from Blackpool Central, they decided to race the "Blackpool lads". As they rattled along on the approach to Kirkham, Len Dickey had given his new 75XXX class 4 locomotive "the gun"; apparently they'd already been told off earlier in the same day for speeding with the new engine having failed to stick to the 60mph speed limit. Len nipped across to Ray's side to watch the Blackpool crew coming off the coast line with their Royal Scot Class loco. On the two trains ran, neck and neck through Kirkham Station and on towards Salwick. Beyond Salwick No.2 signalbox, on the approach to Lea Road troughs, Len looked across at Ray "Get yer sen ready" and with that, Ray slammed the firehole shut then stuck the shovel in the pile of nutty slack in the tender before standing next to the water scoop handle. "Stand by" shouted Len as both engines passed the Springfield works. Len new only too well that there would be little space in the tender tank for much water, but Len had other ideas in mind. As the two trains hit the troughs Len "dropped the wheel" and with it, the roar at the chimney top changed instantly and the train surged forward with the engine behaving like a dog pulling on its lead as they began to overtake the Scot. "Let her go", shouted Len. Down went the scoop, the tender tank became all but full in a matter of seconds, up came the surge of water and the backlash cascaded over

Royal Train 14.4.55. Accrington men, driver Charlie Terry and his young mate fireman Raymond Thorpe stand in front of their loco. No.**90127** before taking th stock of the Royal train from Accrington to Colne in April 1955. Ray was Charlie' regular mate from being 16 until he was 23. Even when he did National Service Charlie still sent Ray 5/- a week, treating him just like a father. (below) One c the new 75's sits on No.8 road at Accrington. *Ray Thorpe / Frank Watson*

the tender back, "a miniature Niagara Falls.....!" Both Ray and Le curled up with laughter as they leaned over the fireman's side. Th backlash of water had hit the Blackpool men's Royal Scot amidship drenching them through in the process, and they were clearly n amused ...! Neil Godwin's mate Driver Percy Horsfield did a similar thing en-route to Blackpool with Crab 2-6-0 No.42727. He and Neil were having a rough time of it, they were "tramming" the old girl flat out along to Lea Road, the regulator was "up in the roof" and the big ends were knocking so hard that both men had to stand up and even then the seats were coming up to meet them with every thump! When it came to putting the scoop in Percy shouted across to Neil, "leave the beggar in, maybe that'll bring a smile to your face" and with that both men looked back down the front coach and laughed as the compartment windows flew up one by one in the wake of the water overflow. Young Neil was a native of Great Harwood and he would soon leave the footplate to go driving on the roads, much to his regret in later years. So many of these young experienced firemen would leave the railway as little in the way of promotion and better wages were on offer. Neil would push-bike or walk across to Rishton from Great Harwood when working late nights or early mornings and Arthur Ratcliffe, the Rishton signalman would slow a passing goods train, to let Neil get a lift down to Church and Oswaldtwistle platform where he'd drop off as the train drifted quietly though in the dark and a short walk then followed past Church East signal box onto the shed.

(above left, centre & right) **Accrington Men (2).** In the early 1950s we see (left to right) young Neil Godwin (fireman) by the coal stage in 1953, and two views of a well known passed man Lawson Peel, on the platform at "Church and Ossie" and later en-route to Wakefield working a passenger job. *Neil Godwin / Raymond Thorpe.*

Accrington Men (1) 25.8.55. On the shed shunt we see "A" class tank No.**51390** and in the cab is Herbert Dobson (right-hand figure). As you may recall Herbert "Was full of Eastern promise" *Brian E Morrison.*

Portrait of a Driver. Charlie Terry "One of the old school", a man for whom fireman Raymond Thorpe had the greatest respect. The engine was No.**42717** and the place was Midge Hall near Preston. The picture was taken in the mid 1950s.
Raymond Thorpe.

Men and Machines. On the "Up side" shunt in the early 1950s are Accrington driver Jimmy Broughton. Behind him young fireman Mark Marshall and on the "floor" is shunter Charlie Shorrock. The loco is "A" class 0-6-0 No.**52529**.
Mark Marshall

Shed Outing 1957. Accrington shed staff in keeping with many other sheds at the time always had an annual outing in the 1950s. These trips were organised by Jack Shackleton from 1952 onwards and below we see the 1957 outing. Those taking part are listed below. (back row) Dennis Hacking, Jack Norris, Jack Knowles, Arnold Greaterix, Archie Johnstone, Bill Rostron, Fred Whitemoss, Alec Woods, Harry South, Bob Shackleton, (on the middle row) John Mcdermot, Herbert Dewhurst, Lol ? , (blacksmith), Jack Shackleton (organiser), Fred Ingham, Albert ? , (steamraiser), John Deveraux, Jack Snape, (steamraiser), T. Lambert, Sammy Edwards. (on the front row), ? , (fitter), Joe Merchant, Bernard Jones, Joe Grime, Albert Dowling, Harry Kenyon, Joe ?, (boilermaker), ? , (fitter), Eddy Lane and finally Johnny Fox.
(courtesy of Mark Marshall).

Church East. passing Church East signalbox a westbound freight heads towards Church and Oswaldtwistle station which is situated just behind the camera. The engine sheds are to the right out of the picture, the carriage sheds etc. can be seen behind the back of the signalbox, in the distance. *Dave Dyson.*

Church and Oswaldtwistle station.

It was shortly after passing Church East signal cabin that we entered the platform at Church and Oswaldtwistle station. Here on both sides of the station there were two mill lodges, so big that they looked like reservoirs. They covered a wide area and no doubt were very deep, but that didn't seem to deter the many kids we used to see climbing about the wood, and later concrete, jetty that edged out into the water near to the up platform of the station. Behind the Down side platform a cobbled yard and sidings formed the little goods yard and the goods warehouse itself was part of the station back wall to which the short platform awning was attached. A wooden station building also sat on the platform as a waiting room, although it always looked slightly out of place. At the platform end a subway building not unlike that at Colne covered the staircase down to the main road below. The most memorable feature I recall of the Down platform was the size of the edging stones. They were quite long but narrow blocks of dressed stone, very unusual and totally different from those on the Up side platform which were the normal large slab type coping. The main station buildings over on the Up side could well be called typically East Lancashire Railway design, of dressed stone, the style of windows and roof being similar to the East Lancashire Rly. buildings at

Church and Oswaldtwistle Station. This time we see an eastbound empty wagon train as it clatters through the platforms at Church and "Ossie". The two towns were situated one on each side of the railway, Church was to the right as we headed for Blackburn, whilst Oswaldtwistle was to the left. *Dave Dyson.*

Accrington. The station awning was an integral part of the slate roof. At the Rishton end of the platform the main road passed beneath the railway. Here the gable end of the Station Hotel was located against the corner of the bridge. A large hoarding high on the gable advertised both Thwaites Ale and the Station Hotel. The station was again one of those that we would rarely stop at until the 1960s, certainly the Sunday specials from Colne at the holidays would call there, particularly the Southport trips, but through the week it was a case of being whisked through the station as our driver made a "dab" at the bank to Rishton. Crossing the viaduct, the line curved away to the right past Blythes Sidings, where a busy scrap dock was always in operation. Behind the sidings across the main road, Blythes chemical plant churned out enough obnoxious smells to make your eyes water. Also on the Down side of the line at this point were the tar distillers Metcalfes, and outside their works it was possible to see examples of the ancient square tank tar wagons. Painted black, these old short wheel based wagons probably dated back to L.&Y. days and were often to be seen being shunted or taken up towards Accrington to the main goods despatch point. Across the way on the Up line was Aspen Colliery signal cabin. This block post controlled the sidings nearby including Metcalfes. Behind the signal cabin had been the Colliery itself and though long gone certain relics of this industrial site still remained such as the nearby coke ovens that were built in the banking side.

Church Bank to Daisyfield Junction.

We would now be climbing Church Bank, heading away from the built up area of Accrington and out into the countryside once more. The Leeds to Liverpool Canal is still with us as it had been since approaching Burnley. Weaving its way back and forth by the railway, it now appeared on our right hand side as we looked out across the fields to the valley and hills beyond. Over beyond the canal bridges and the deep valley below lay Great Harwood, on the loop line to Padiham, its towering gasometers clearly visible. Occasionally we would see the exhaust of a passing steam train as it climbed the bank from Martholme viaduct up to Great Harwood station, the locomotive's white exhaust leaving a steady trail along the valley side in the fresh morning air. Our own engine wasn't fairing too badly either, it was doing its share of barking as we climbed the 1 in 132 bank past Rishton golf course. An overbridge signified the entry to Rishton, and it was here that the goods yard could be seen on the right as we leaned to the left hand curve on the run into the station. If we were to call at Rishton, the drivers usually shut off steam passing the overbridge and allowed the gradient to slow us and we would gently roll into the station needing only a light application of the brake to bring us to a stand. More often than not we would rattle through Rishton in fine style, whistling as we flashed by the platforms before heading for the overbridge and short tunnel beyond. In later years, as with other smaller stations, we would always tend to call at Rishton despite only picking up a handful of passengers.

Rishton station.

The station here was quite "bonnie", being very rural looking and you wouldn't have thought that it lay so close to both Accrington and Blackburn. Even the main station buildings tended to look more like a large farmhouse than a railway structure. They were made of random stone and they looked very solid indeed. The goods warehouse, again a large random stone affair, was attached to these fine station buildings, looking for all the world like the barn that matched the farmhouse. The signalbox was ideally situated on the Down platform near the warehouse and afforded good views of the line in both directions. The original signal box had been positioned next to the overbridge at the Accrington end of Rishton. It was a tall red brick affair and appears to have been abandoned because of movement of the foundations. However, the blackened brick base of the box could be seen close to the bridge for many years. A long metal lattice foot bridge spanned all the goods yard and the main lines, giving access to the platforms - (not unlike the footbridge at nearby Great Harwood station). The booking office was situated near the main gate some distance from the actual platforms. Next to the booking office, the Railway Hotel was a handy source of refreshment. Beneath the foot bridge the cobbled road access to the goods yard was usually piled high with coal and a number of coal merchants operated from the sidings here. You'd see them busily bagging up the "nutty slack"

Blythes Sidings. Beyond the station at Church and Oswaldtwistle the private sidings and scrap loading dock known as Blythes sidings were situated. In this picture No.**44940** passes Metcalfes, the tar distillers (note the tar wagons in the left background). On the extreme left is Aspen Colliery signalbox. Blythes Sidings were to be found just to the right of the engine bufferbeam. *Geoff Robinson*

wearing their leather waistcoats with the metal studs in them, looking like Roman gladiators in flat caps.... ! Over on the Up platform the buildings were of red brick, with a traditional roof of blue slate, they comprised waiting and ladies rooms together with gents toilets which were positioned further along at the Blackburn end of the platform. However, these toilets were made of random stone rather than brick. Neat little flower beds with white painted brick surrounds adorned both platforms and clearly the station was a picture on bright summer days. The Blackburn end of Rishton would see a small cattle dock over on the right standing by the loop which was formed by the line passing through the goods warehouse. This loop continued down in the Blackburn direction towards the overbridge, beyond which lay Rishton Tunnel. This was only a short tunnel which carried the main road at an angle above the railway. Looking ahead the signals showed Rishton's "starter" and the distant signal for Whitebirk East. The gradient fell as we headed towards Rishton tunnel, it was now down hill all the way to Blackburn.

Accrington Holidays. (above). No.**44949** working an Accrington to Fleetwood excursion 1T70 at Accrington holidays runs into the platform at Rishton on a very sunny 28th July 1963. (*below*). Platform access at Rishton was via an early ornate type of latticed footbridge constructed by the L. & Y. Railway. This long footbridge spanned all the lines in the goods yard as well as the main line, but passengers tended to use the barrow crossing as they made their way to and from the main gate rather than climbing the steps of the footbridge.

Geoff Robinson / S. Taylor.

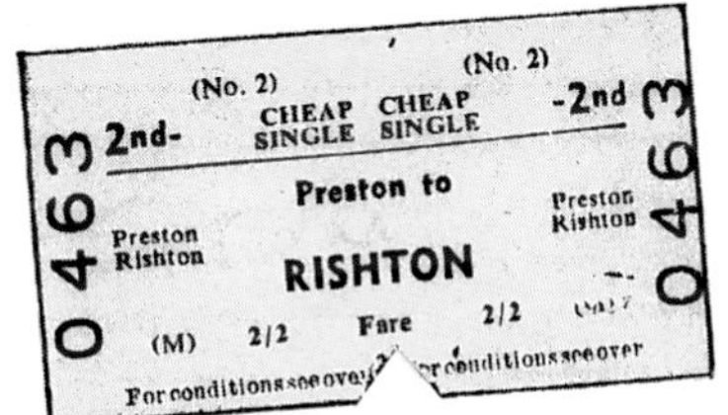

Entering Rishton. No.45068 working 1T76 a Colne to Fleetwood excursion enters the Up platform at Rishton station, having just come up the bank from Accrington on a warm summer's morning (9th June 1963). *Geoff Robinson.*

Rishton Station (1). The rather unusual main structure looked more like a farm building especially with the goods shed being attached and having an arched entrance for rail traffic, the whole affair resembled more a farmhouse and barn than a goods warehouse and station building. *S.Taylor.*

No big rail rush from Rishton

1961

Though definite figures are not known at the moment, there appears to be no great rush compared with previous years in holidaymakers travelling from Rishton.

The Station Master (Mr. J. Weir) said that, as usual, the most popular seaside resort was Blackpool.

There are quite a number of people who have booked on the 9-16 a.m. and the 1-52 p.m. trains to Blackpool.

Long distance resorts — Bournemouth, Yarmouth, Newquay and Brighton—are going rather slowly at the moment, though bookings are expected to pick up a little for weekend.

Douglas (I-o-M.) runs next in line for popularity to Blackpool. Bookings are going quite well, and this, again, is expected to pick up by weekend.

The North Wales resorts are proving popular. There are quite a number of bookings for Llandudno, though Bangor seems to be going slowly.

Rishton holidaymakers have relied on the old "faithful," Blackpool, and are taking advantage of the cheap period return fare (7s. 3d.)

Rishton Station (2). Rishton's signalbox was positioned upon the Down platform. The comfort of the box is well remembered by Neil Godwin who spent many happy times there talking with signalman Arthur Ratcliffe as he waited for an early morning lift on a freight train down to the loco. sheds at Accrington.. *S.Taylor.*

(above). **Rishton. 20.6.64.** Stanier "big 8" No.**48080** hoists a train of empties over the top at Rishton station, as it heads back to the Yorkshire coalfields. Unlike the Down side platform "farm" type buildings the Up side were a more traditional design in red brick. The rural beauty of the station is very evident in this view. (below) A pair of "Accrington" sets leave for Blackburn on this lovely summer's day in June 1964. *Geoff Robinson*

Gathering speed, we rushed on past the two feeder reservoirs which erved the Leeds to Liverpool Canal, which by now was below us in he direction of the Harwood loop line. These feeder reservoirs be-ame increasingly popular over the years with dinghy sailors. Our un into Blackburn from here could well be slow and by the time we ad passed Whitebirk East, the brakes were on and the speed fell apidly. We had joined the queue of trains waiting to use Blackburn unnel, our line plus the Harwood loop and the line from Hellifield. vhich came in at Daisyfield, would all have some sort of extra serv-ces travelling over them at this time of year so we were often delayed. Jnconcerned, mum would be busy reading the paper , talking of mak-ng a brew whilst dad would lightly tap another Player's "ciggy" on he outside of his battered cigarette case, the same one that he'd car-ied in the Western Desert in the last war, and satisfied that both ends vere right, he'd flick the lid of his old lighter, then light up before aking his usual stance in the carriage doorway as we rolled gently ast the large power station at Whitebirk. The slow run into Blackburn ave us ample time to survey the surroundings at Whitebirk. The coal torage point for the power station lay on the opposite side of the anal to the power plant. The canal crossed beneath the railway at ght angles at this point. Coal, as at Huncoat power plant, was trans-erred across to the power station by covered conveyer belts and for any years, even in the 1960s, coal would still arrive at Whitebirk by anal barge. Special grab cranes were situated on the canal bank and ey hoisted the coal onto a dock area from which it was moved onto the conveyer. The tall boiler-house chimneys and the cooling towers stood quite close to the railway banking and the goods loops where the coal trains shunted into the sidings would continue down towards Whitebirk West signal box. From here on into Blackburn the scene

continued on page 103

Whitebirk Power Station

Whitebirk East. No.**45205**, working 1Z13 a Colne to Blackpool "Halfex", passes the signal box and power station sidings at Whitebirk East on the run down to Blackburn. *Dave Dyson.*

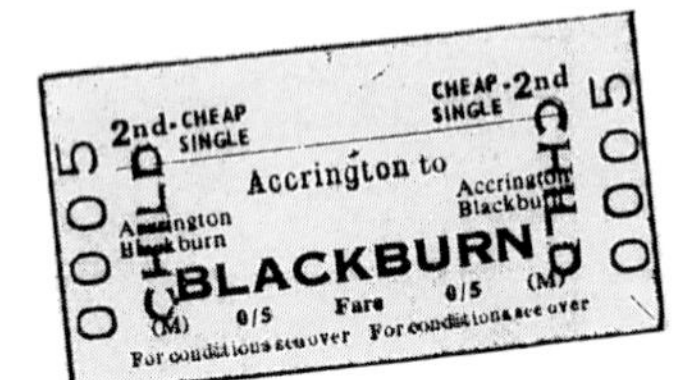

Whitebirk West 7.10.62. Another pair of "Accrington" sets (DMU's) speed down the bank towards Great Harwood Junction passing en-route the large structure of Whitebirk power station. (below) No.**42878** of Lower Darwen, runs light towards Whitebirk, to the left of the picture is the "Northrop" loom factory at Great Harwood Jnc., (where the wind howled) and in front of the engine in the field over towards the Harwood loop line there was always a "Hall's Distemper" sign visible from both the main line and the loop. *Geoff Robinson.*

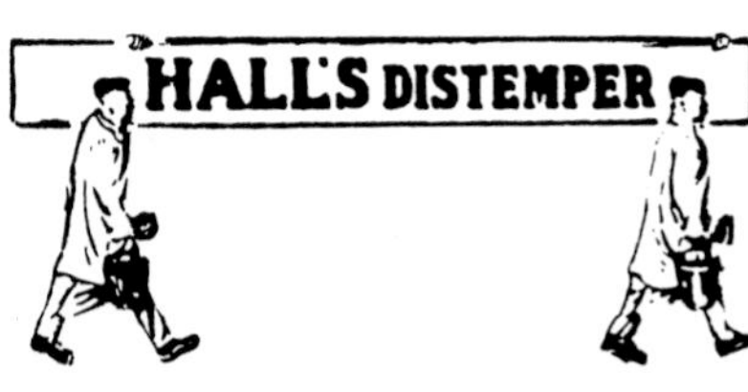

Evening
BLACKPOOL 4/3

	Sat 15 July	Sat 22 July	Sat 29 July
Depart	p.m.	p.m.	p.m.
ACCRINGTON .	4.35	4.37	4.35
CHURCH & O ..	4.40	4.40	4.40
Return	p.m.	p.m.	p.m.
Blackpool C .	11.20	11.20	11.10

Great Harwood Junction. No.**44870** with another 1Z13 special rattles past the Junction signalbox. the Northrop foundry is seen to the left of the picture, whilst on the right are the loops and Greenbank Gasworks sidings.
Noel Coates

(below). **"Putting the Black into Blackburn"!** This used to happen if you shut the firehole doors too soon. The lack of draught prevents proper combustion. No.**45275** of Rose Grove with a good belly full of fire climbs away from Daisyfield past the other part of the Northrop works. Daisyfield Junction is just beyond the bridge in the distance.
Noel Coates.

became more and more industrial, piles of coal, literally hundreds of tons of it lined the railway, these stockpiles being dumped on a vast waste area close to Greenbank gasworks. The pungent smell of sulphur and coal gas lingered heavily in the air at this point. Close by there were goods lines and sidings from which the coal was supplied and these were to be seen opposite Great Harwood Junction signal box.

The signal box sat right on the Junction of the lines from Great Harwood and Rishton and quite often the signalmen here tended to give preference to the Rishton route and occasionally, as we passed this point there would be another excursion train in the shallow cutting at the end of the Padiham - Great Harwood loop line " champing at the bit ",waiting for a run into Blackburn.

The British Northop Loom Co.,

Running down from Whitebirk you couldn't help but see the large letters NORTHOP, painted in white, on the side of the modern red brick factory building. A number of large factory buildings comprised the huge Northop Loom complex at Philips Road in Blackburn. It wasn't really possible from the railway to tell just how big the scale of things were at Northop, for the factory area stretched for acres around Whitebirk. The building mentioned earlier with the name painted on it was set at an angle towards the railway and was perched somewhat higher up than the line. When passing Great Harwood Junction and this building, a wind tunnel effect was created and a rushing sound roared beneath the carriages on the train, this sound continuing for about a minute until we had travelled past the Northop gable end. Even in the pitch black of night when returning home it was still possible to know where we were as soon as the wind rush started. The huge Northop foundry, said to be the largest of its type in Europe , ran parallel to the railway for some considerable distance towards Daisyfield Junction. At the end of the foundry a large makeshift car park, with a surface of boiler ash and clinker, separated the other portion of the works which was a two storey mill close to Daisyfield. A few rows of terraced houses had formally occupied the car park site, covering all the ground right up to the railway embankment. These houses had been pulled down in the mid 1950s and now just a few gaily painted red brick terraces were to be seen further back some distance from the railway. Clearly the workers at Northop were earning wages good enough to support the purchase and operation of a motor vehicle even in the 'fifties. The firm started in 1902 and the works at Philips Road began in 1907, eventually 2000 workers being employed. In the firms heyday, these workers were producing 10,000 looms a year, many of which were for export. They had successfully pioneered the worlds first fully automatic loom and 44,000 of these had been made by 1933. You could say that they played an important roll in the decline of the Lancashire cotton industry, by exporting so many modern looms. The real facts were however, that the old mill owners in our areas would just not spend their hard earned cash modernising their mills, preferring to potter along using the old traditional " Lanky " looms from the last century . By the 1960s only a thousand workers remained at Northop and the decline in the 60s from then on was steady. By the end of the decade large sections of the Northop works had closed and the end was in sight.

Daisyfield and Blackburn Tunnel.

Rolling past the Northop works the rumble of the coaching stock would echo as we became hemmed in by high mills on both sides of the line near to Daisyfield Junction. A little coal yard was situated to the right with a head shunt which extended up under the brick overbridge by the Northop mill. We were now approaching the junction with the line from Hellifield, and round the corner to the right but some distance away we could see the tiny level crossing and station together with the little signal cabin at Daisyfield. Around the station area was a community of blackened red brick terraced houses, their many chimneys adding to the already murky Blackburn air. Daisyfield Junction signal box stood guard over the junction itself and a number of sidings sat behind the box here. Across on the Up side was the busy timber yard of Messrs. Evans - later to become Southern Evans; here again a number of sidings sat close to the yard. Private sidings ran both into the wood yard and across the nearby lane into the mill yard some distance from the main lines. Approaching Blackburn tunnel, we began to drop into a slight cutting, where above us on both sides there were more blackened rows of terraced houses. We could see as we crept past them that they were sadly run down, the sash windows having small panes of glass in them which were filthy, no doubt from the passage of dozens of steam engines. Curtains hanging in the windows looked equally ready for a wash. The actual approach to Blackburn tunnel seemed very daunting for, perched high above it was a three or four storey mill and even further skywards was a large mill chimney, which was merrily churning out a load of dirty brown "Fug", so much for the Clean Air Act! As we prepared to be swallowed up by the tunnel, we could see the smoke still rising from the tunnel mouth following the passage of the previous train. The engine just in front of us was by now close to the tunnel mouth and would give a watery shriek on the whistle, at which point dad would announce in an authoritative voice "Blagburn Tunnel". Just where the term "Blagburn" came from I never did find out, but this was the sort of slang Dad used and having voiced where we were, he proceeded to yank up the droplight window by pulling on the thick leather strap. No sooner had the window banged shut than we were plunged into the smoky depths of the tunnel. Progress was slow and outside the compartment window, on which condensation was quickly forming, we could just about make out the occasional glimpse of the sulphur-coated tunnel wall as the smoke from the engine drifted past the compartment window. Inside the coach the dim light in the roof flickered and every now and then little lights would also appear on the tunnel walls outside. The tunnel seemed endless as on we rumbled ,the noise of the big solid wheels under the coach echoing in this dark domain. Just when it seemed that the tunnel would never end , the blackness turned to grey as the light from the tunnel mouth loomed ahead.

British Northrop Loom Co. Ltd.
Philips Road
Blackburn

Northrop Workers. Creating textile machinery in Lancashire for export abroad to countries who bought cloth from us was a recipe for disaster and in the end, even the Northrop works paid the price and by the 1960s the last 1000 or so workers would join the dole queues.

Daisyfield Junction and Blackburn Tunnel. It was here that the line from Hellifield and Clitheroe curved in to join us on our right side. We came to know the area around Daisyfield very well. Having crept down from Harwood Junction, we would now have to wait until the preceding excursions had loaded passengers in Blackburn station. The area was full of smoky terrace houses and the cobbled streets gave this part of Blackburn a very real feeling of "Coronation Street" land. In the above picture Low Moor Black 5 No.**44693** is about to clatter over the junction at Daisyfield with 1X18 - a Bradford to Blackpool North working. The Northrop Loom plant is seen behind the train. Over to the left of the engine is the station and level crossing signal box at Daisyfield which were situated just on the Hellifield line.

(*left*). Passing Daisyfield signal box ahead of us we would see rows of cobbled streets and terraced houses as Blackburn tunnel beckoned.

Our last look at the east end of Blackburn tunnel shows the tunnel mouth and the large red brick mill which sat above it. Smoke was often still pouring out of the tunnel mouth from the passage of the preceding excursions and visibility was frequently very poor. On one occasion two Illumination specials, returning to Yorkshire, collided near the tunnel, one running smack into the rear of the other. Excursions were running nose to tail that particular night and total chaos prevailed for hours.

Noel Coates (2) G.H.Platt (1)

West End of Blackburn Tunnel. Emerging from the black hole, into Blackburn station, we would quickly become accustomed to the bright light, ready to collect the numbers of the local pilot engine, etc., such as No.**44460** seen below. This loco was subject to two excellent photographs taken in May 1961, the one on this page, adjacent to the newly re-decked Fish Dock, also appearing in the Spring 1964 Ian Allan Combined volume. *G.H. Platt and R.S. Greenwood.*

Blackburn Tunnel 25.8.55. The exit into the bright sunlight, was most welcome, after the smoky atmosphere of the tunnel. No.**42481** clatters over the points bringing a semi-fast into the station.
Brian E Morrison.

:eproduced here are sections of the Spring 1964 edition of Ian Allan's combined olume with County Class loco at Penzance on the front cover. Richard Green- vood's picture is seen at the top of the picture page. The main views on this page ıow (above) Class 5 No.**45109** arriving at Blackburn on 28th August 1964 on a 'olne to Manchester working. The Fish Dock can be seen to the extreme left of ıe picture. The picture below, taken in May 1961 on the same day as the com- ined volume study, shows No.**44460** alongside No.1 platform, with the stock of ıe 10.19am to Hellifield (9.20am ex Manchester Victoria).

Bert Holland / R.S. Greenwood.

E. L. Yard & Fish Dock

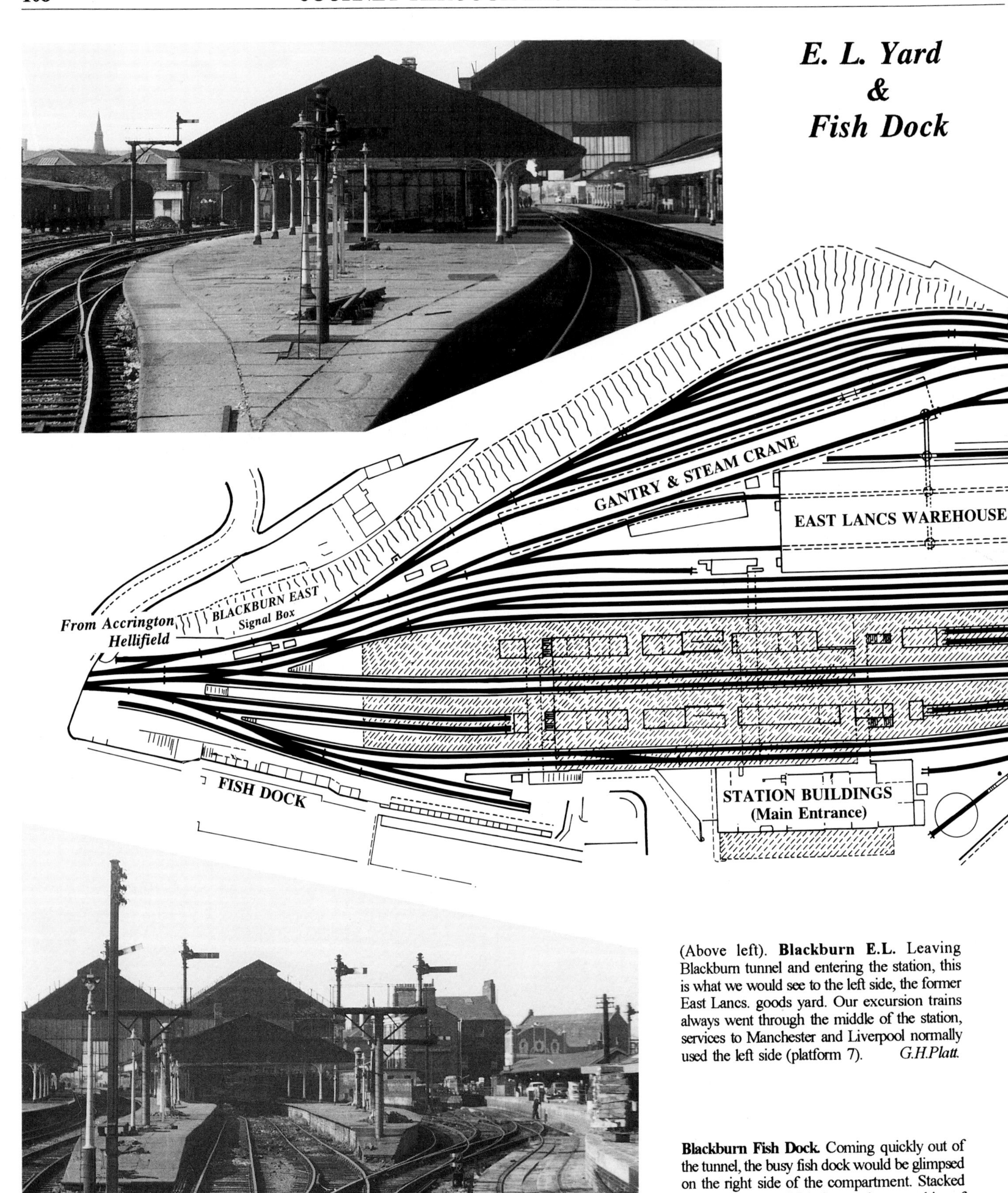

(Above left). **Blackburn E.L.** Leaving Blackburn tunnel and entering the station, this is what we would see to the left side, the former East Lancs. goods yard. Our excursion trains always went through the middle of the station, services to Manchester and Liverpool normally used the left side (platform 7). *G.H.Platt.*

Blackburn Fish Dock. Coming quickly out of the tunnel, the busy fish dock would be glimpsed on the right side of the compartment. Stacked high with boxes of fish, it was always an hive of activity in a morning. Many traders seem to have "lock - ups", a sort of open market for fish. *G.H.Platt.*

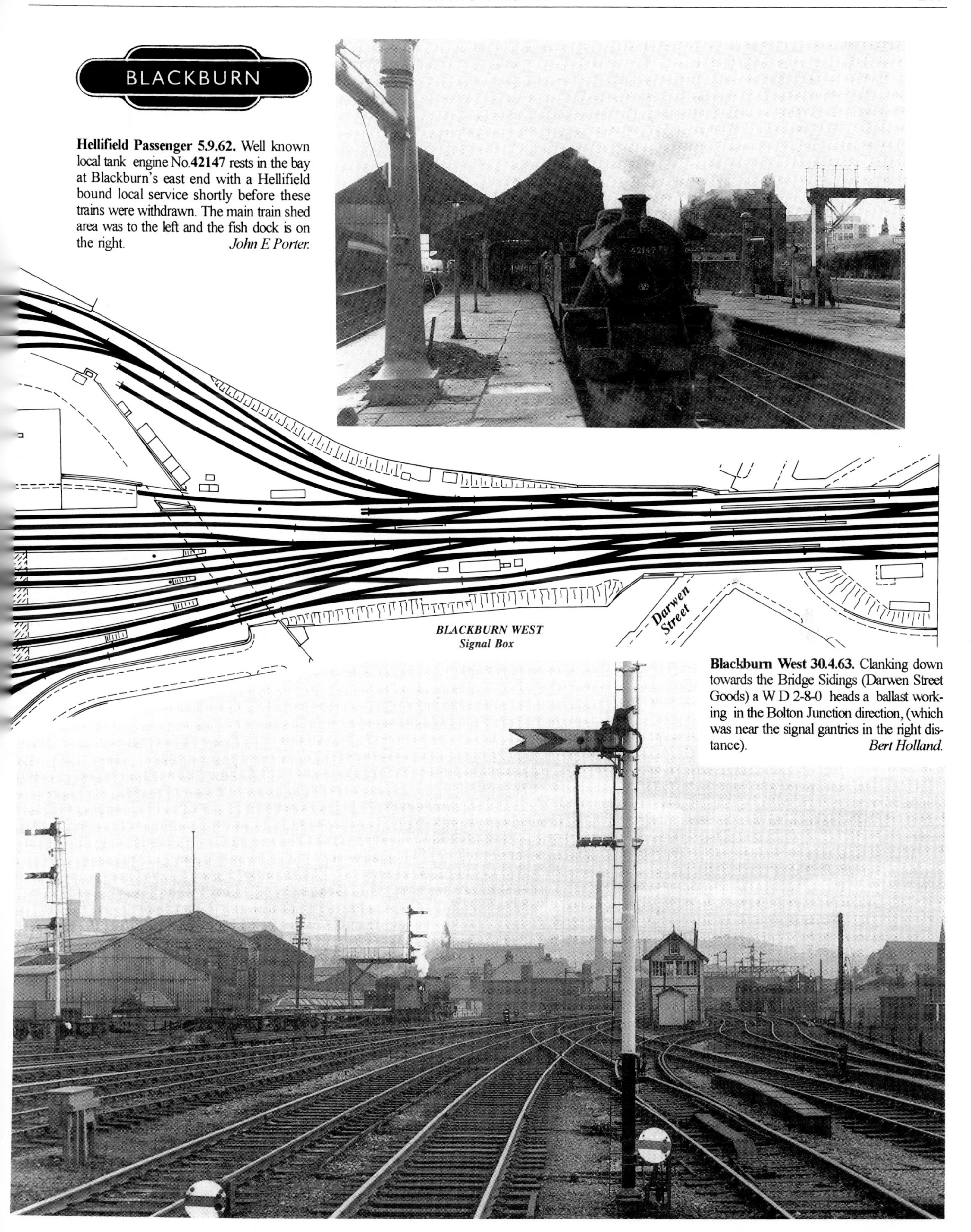

Hellifield Passenger 5.9.62. Well known local tank engine No.**42147** rests in the bay at Blackburn's east end with a Hellifield bound local service shortly before these trains were withdrawn. The main train shed area was to the left and the fish dock is on the right. *John E Porter.*

Blackburn West 30.4.63. Clanking down towards the Bridge Sidings (Darwen Street Goods) a W D 2-8-0 heads a ballast working in the Bolton Junction direction, (which was near the signal gantries in the right distance). *Bert Holland.*

(above) the last ever working L.. & Y. Rly. signal. *Peter Fitton.*

DOUGLAS
(via Fleetwood)
SUNDAYS until 20th AUGUST

Hapton	dep	9.09 a.m	28/6
Huncoat	dep	9.12 a.m.	28/3
Accrington ...	dep	9.20 a.m.	27/9
Church & O..	dep	9.22 a.m.	27/9

Second Class Rail and First Class Steamer — Fare 4/- extra
Bookings also to Fleetwood

Blackburn Station - a cathedral like place!

On the Platform. The familar "Lanky" train indicator boards were still in use in July 1962 as we see here on Blackburn's No.2 platform. (above right). The last-ever working L & Y signal was to be found over by the wall side near No.1 platform. The shunt arms here were used particularly on a Saturday when the two portions of the Glasgow train were coupled together, (the Liverpool and Manchester portions). (right) This beautiful model of the M.V. Viking graced platform 2 throughout the 1950s and 60s. The Viking herself was still at sea until the end of the 1954 summer season.

G.H.Platt. S.Taylor. Peter Fitton.

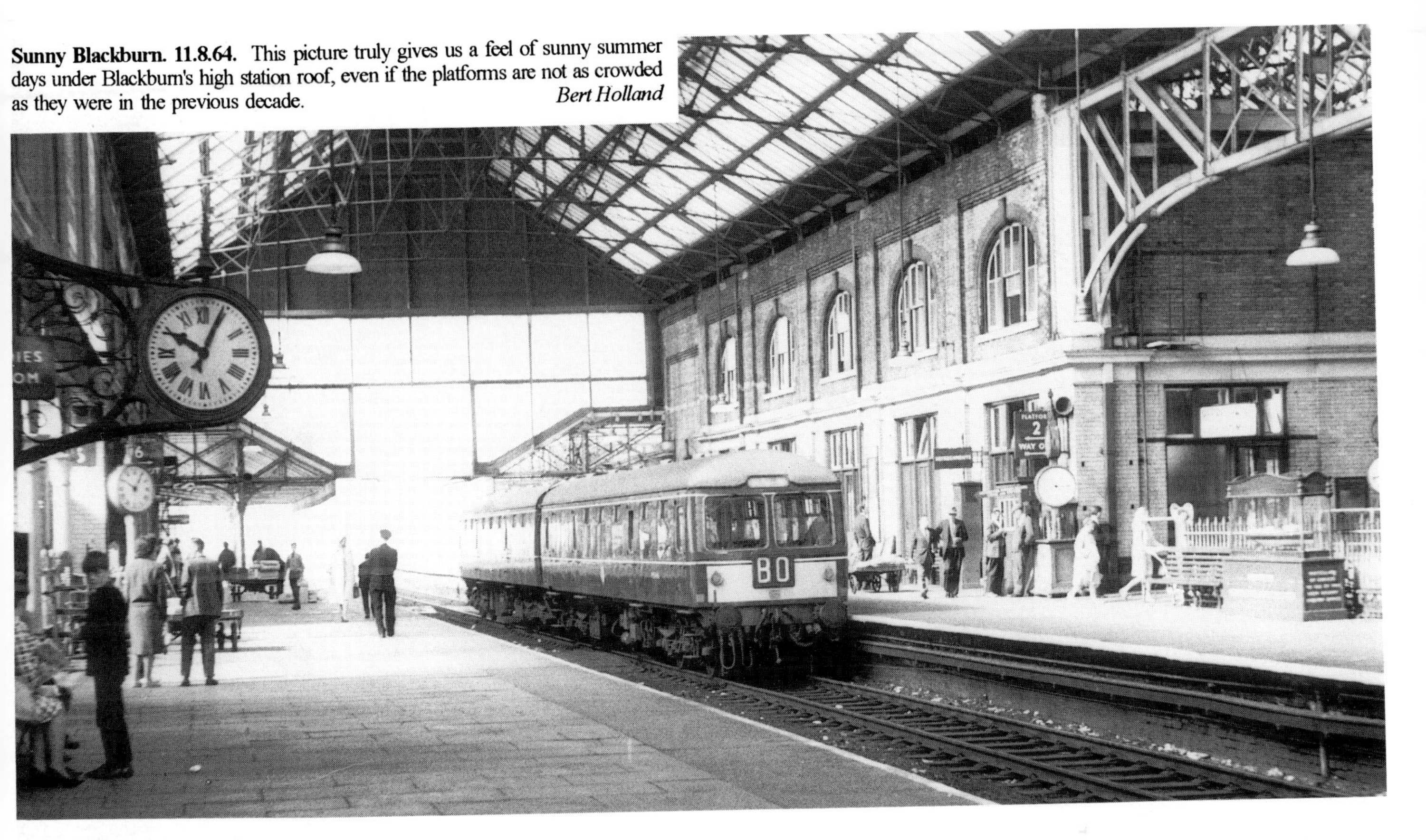

Sunny Blackburn. 11.8.64. This picture truly gives us a feel of sunny summer days under Blackburn's high station roof, even if the platforms are not as crowded as they were in the previous decade. *Bert Holland*

Blackburn station.

The exit from Blackburn tunnel would come quickly. Suddenly out of the smoky depths we'd be thrust into the dazzling summer sun. The compartment windows were quickly dropped to catch a glimpse of the station approaches. The fish dock always attracted our attentions, it was such an hive of activity. It was located over to the right with an unloading dock which ran almost up to the tunnel mouth. Men in flat caps and white aprons busily wheeled truck loads of fish boxes around the platform there and a number of large weigh-scales were in use and the various traders had name boards up above their lock-ups. Road vehicles also parked on the loading dock . Passing the fish dock also gave us a look at the east bay platforms where now and again the Whalley bank engine would be sitting, possibly getting water. Locos. such as No.44460 and the B.R. Standard 2-6-0's Nos.76080-84 would share the banking turns together with the odd Crab 2-6-0's like Nos.42729 and 42732. Over on the left at this point was the Blackburn East signalbox, a large timber framed box with an unusual crossed framed timber base to the front elevation. The large sidings and ware-house of the former East Lancs. Railway sat further to our left and adjacent to us was the main Manchester platform which curved round the outside of the station. We would soon slip beneath the cathedral like roof of the station and as you can imagine with such a high roofed building, every noise seemed to echo, the sound of the coach bogies as they bounced over the rail joints, the chorus of the birds sitting on the girders high above and the laughter and chatter of the crowds thronging the many platforms. Despite the gloom and grime of the train shed, the sun still managed to cast shafts of bright light down through the roof glazing onto the crowded platforms below. As we continued to roll gently through the platform we tended to ignore the sea of faces flashing past on the platform side and instead our attentions focussed on the large glass case with the model boat inside it, which always sat by the subway railings on platform 5. This was used to promote the sailings from Liverpool and Heysham to the Isle of Man and Belfast etc. Displaying these model boats had long been a tradition, certainly dating back to LMS days, and a number of these boats in glass cabinets would advertise such services. It runs in my mind that boats were also displayed at Fleetwood on the timber-floored concourse there and also in the ornate station buildings at Morecambe Promenade. These glass display cabinets promoted the sailings of the Isle of Man Steam Packet Company, a company with a long seafaring tradition. The model to be seen at Blackburn was of course the famous M.V. Viking, possibly their longest serving vessel. It worked the Fleetwood to Douglas run for many years and launched in March 1905, it remained in use until August 1954, before being taken to Thomas Ward's at Barrow in Furness for breaking up. In the glass cabinet there was also a list of other Isle of Man Steam Packet Co. boats which had operated from the turn of the century, including the various vessels which had bore the names of "Ben-My-Chree, Mona's Isle and Mona's Queen". When looking across at the display cabinet here at Blackburn, you couldn't help thinking of the old Liverpool joke about the teacher who asked his class "Who painted the Mona Lisa?" and one little boy replied, "Please sir, Cammell Lairds, they paint all the Isle of Man boats......!" Other memories of Blackburn station would be of the old "Lanky" destination clocks. These were the clock faces where porters used to adjust the hands to show the departure time of the next service. They would then take out a destination sign board from the wooden stand beneath the clock and insert it into a slot at the side of the clock face. On this board would be a full list of the places at which the train would call.

Blackburn Station

The extensive platform buildings at Blackburn were built to a high standard, plenty of good quality wood going into the doors and fittings. Incidentally, the doors leading in to the refreshment rooms ladies and waiting rooms etc. must have been at least 10 to 12 feet high, likewise the ceilings in these rooms, and as a result keeping the rooms warm in winter was a problem. The paintwork throughout the station was a faded red and cream and much of the brickwork was glazed, again in red and cream. The walls in places were very grime encrusted and many of the coloured bricks appeared faded. Nevertheless the station was forever busy, especially at local holiday times. The main platforms were very long indeed, numbers one, five, six and seven holding at least 14 coach lengths, our little nine coach load easily fitting on any of these platforms. Stopping as we did close to the waiting crowd, there was often a surge of people sweeping down towards the engine and our end compartment. Quickly, dad would press his large frame against the lowered window in the compartment door and brother Bert and I would sit tight up to the little side windows to prevent the would-be boarders seeing if there was any room in the compartment. The inquiring persons would come near craning their necks in an effort to see in, the daunting prospect of having to get dad to move soon sending them packing! Whilst all the commotion was going on we'd have time to look over towards the E.L. yard where a large blackened stone warehouse ran parallel to the Number 7 (Manchester) platform. Shunt engines would be busy shuffling to and fro, "hitting" wagons up into the various sidings by the warehouse. More engines could be seen standing down in the distance at Darwen Street bridge, (the long deep girder underbridge). These engines could range from Crabs to Derby 4s, Class 8s to Austerities and Black 5s to Standard 4 2-6-0's. Close by where we were standing, the west bays of the station would become the stabling point for the diesel 350h.p. shunt engines when they took over the shunt duties around Blackburn in the 1960s. Over on the right side of the station (Down side), there was a single line bay platform and over beyond that tucked away around the corner of the main office buildings was a turntable, perched high above street level. This must surely have been a most precarious place to turn a loco. and no wonder there was a big concrete block placed as a bufferstop only a short distance from the 30 to 40 feet drop which overlooked the street below. A good three or four minutes would be taken up loading the many passengers at Blackburn. It is as well to point out that stopping at Blackburn wasn't always the case and as with Accrington, it was more likely the Sunday excursions and those to Southport etc. which would call at the

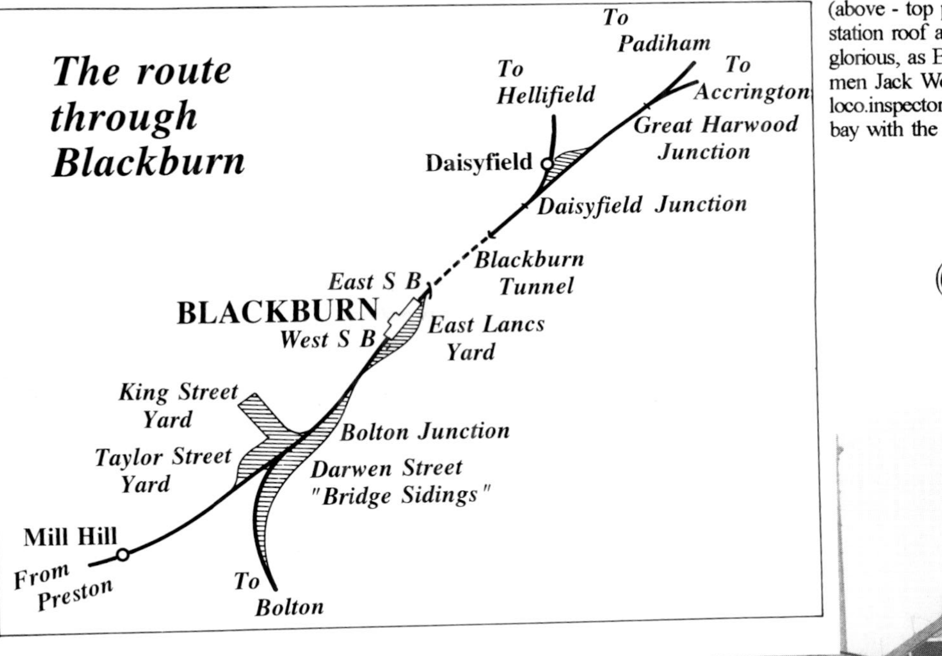

(above - top picture) No.**70013** *Oliver Cromwell* on that fateful last day of steam (11. 8. 68) slips beneath the station roof at Blackburn. That day the crowds really did resemble those of the 1950s, even the weather was glorious, as B.R. ran out of steam. (above - lower picture) The crew on that last journey north were Blackburn men Jack Weal (guard), Raymond Watton (fireman), Bob Grogan (driver) and London Midland Region chief loco.inspector J. Hughes. (below) On an equally sunny summers day 13 years earlier No.**40120** sits in the west bay with the 3.45pm stopping train to Manchester Victoria, the date was 25.8.55.

Ron Graham (2) Brian E Morrison. (1)

BLACKBURN

THE RAILWAY EXECUTIVE
M.78 THIRD CLASS to
FROM Nelson
TO Glasgow & BACK
FOR CONDITIONS SEE BACK

B.R. 14300/300

BRITISH TRANSPORT COMMISSION

Telephone
Our Reference
Your Reference

STATION MASTER
LONDON MIDLAND REGION
BLACKBURN STATION

4th May, 1961.

Master Bernard Bond,
4, St.Cecilia Street,
GT.HARWOOD,
Blackburn.

Dear Master Bond,

I was please to receive your letter of the 3rd May asking for permission to "Train Spot" at this Station.

If you present this letter to the Ticket Collector here you and your friend, Richard Leigh, on purchase of a platform ticket each, will be allowed on the platform so that you may see the passing of 60022 Mallard.

Yours faithfully,

Station Master.

Blackburn Darwen Street (Bridge Sidings)

Darwen Street Goods Yard. Commonly known as Blackburn "Bridge" sidings. This, at one time, was a very busy freight yard. In the above picture the shunters look to be having an L.D.C. meeting outside the shunters cabin, but more than likely they are just having a breather before the arrival of the next goods working that will require "Raffling" (shunting) out. In the entries in the running shift foremans log for Lower Darwen shed, it was amazing the number of times engines were "off" the road (derailed) in these sidings. It was nearly always "Crab " 2-6 -0 's and the modern Ivatt "Doodle bug" types which bit the dust here.....!
British Railways.

Blackburn Bolton Junction

(top picture) **The Long Meg.** No.**92076** passes by Blackburn's Bolton Junction signalbox, with the Long Meg to Widnes Anhydrite train in May 1965. Bolton Junction signalbox is seen in the distance near to Islington Road overbridge. The area to the right by the warehouse is where we'd usually see one of the 76000 types shunting about in the early 1960s. (lower picture) No.**92010** at Tanhouse Lane, Widnes with firemen Vinny Staffa (leaning over cab doors) and fellow Blackburn crewmates in the mid 1960s.

Bert Holland / Vinny Staffa.

The "Long Meg"

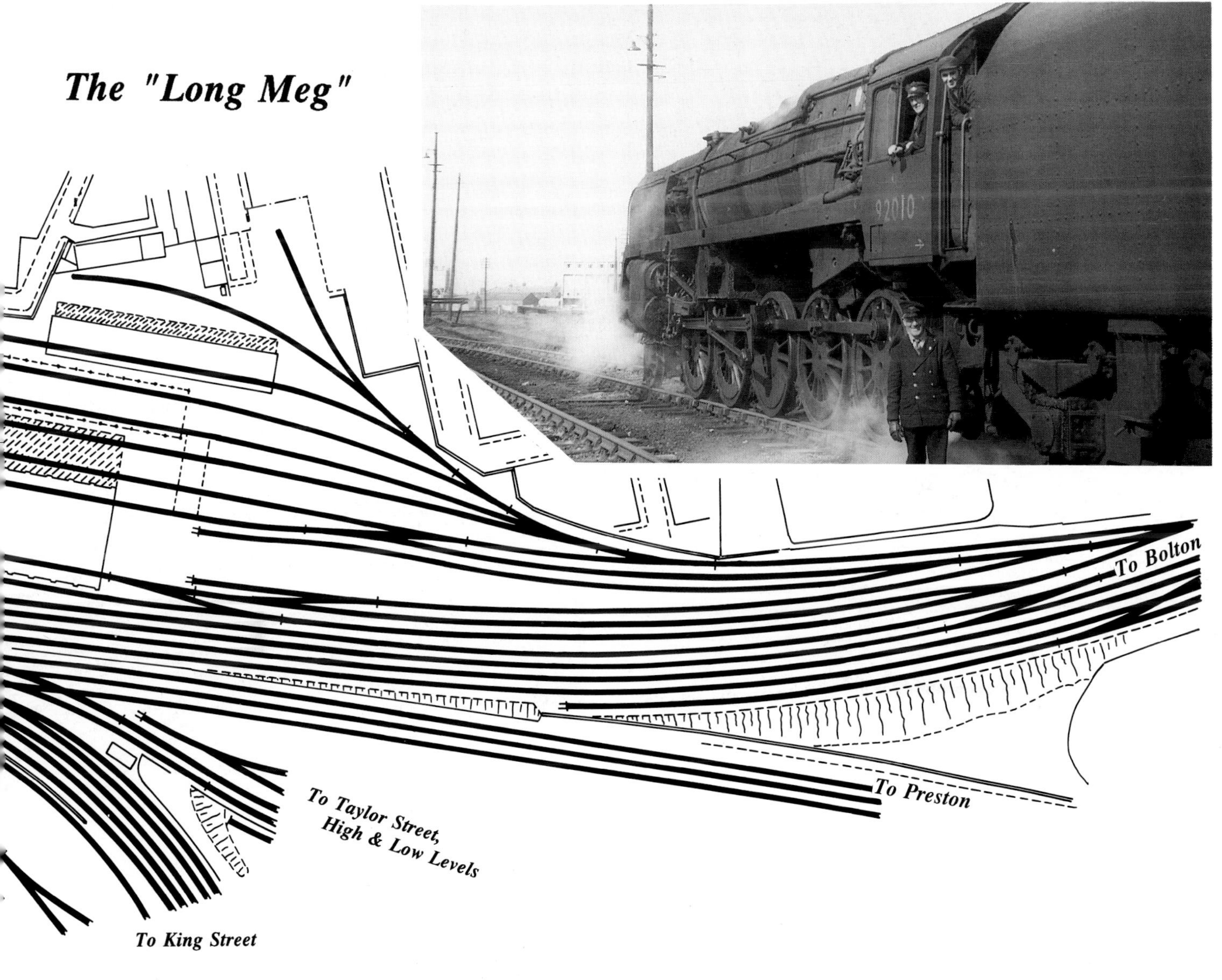

Footplatemen of Lower Darwen M.P.D 24D - Blackburn's local loco shed

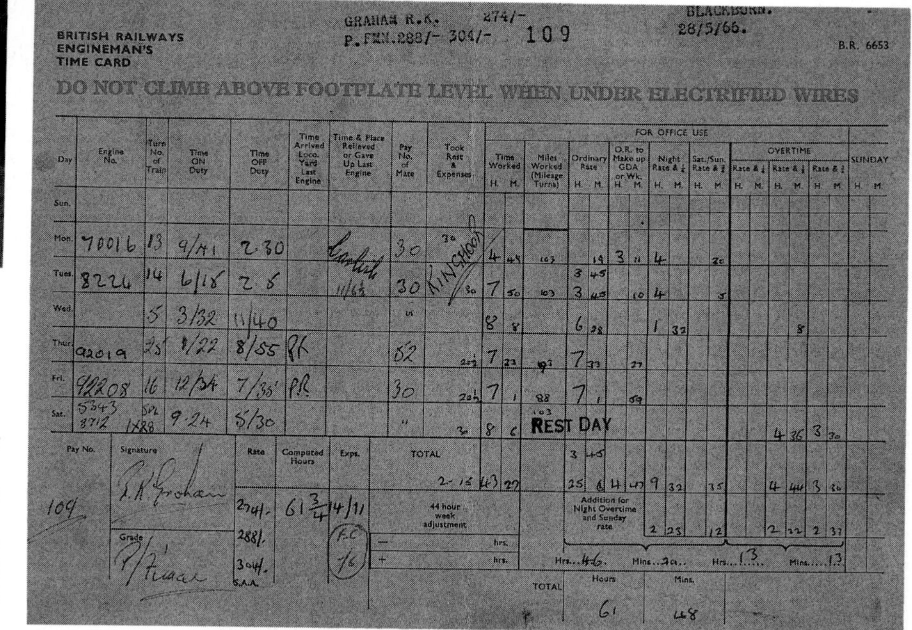

BRITISH RAILWAYS ENGINEMAN'S TIME CARD

GRAHAM R.K. 274/-
P.FMN.288/- 304/- 109

BLACKBURN.
28/5/66.

B.R. 6653

DO NOT CLIMB ABOVE FOOTPLATE LEVEL WHEN UNDER ELECTRIFIED WIRES

Day	Engine No.	Turn No. of Train	Time ON Duty	Time OFF Duty	Time Arrived Loco. Yard Last Engine	Time & Place Relieved or Gave Up Last Engine	Pay No. of Mate	Took Rest & Expenses	Time Worked H.	Time Worked M.	Miles Worked (Mileage Turns)	Ordinary Rate H.	Ordinary Rate M.	O.R. to Make up GDA or Wk. H.	O.R. to Make up GDA or Wk. M.	Night Rate & ¼ H.	Night Rate & ¼ M.	Sat./Sun. Rate & ½ H.	Sat./Sun. Rate & ½ M.	Overtime Rate & ¼ H.	Overtime Rate & ¼ M.	Overtime Rate & ½ H.	Overtime Rate & ½ M.	Overtime Rate & ½ H.	Overtime Rate & ½ M.	Sunday H.	Sunday M.
Sun.																											
Mon.	70016	13	9/41	2.30		Carlisle	30	30 KINGMOOR	4	44	103		19	3	11	4			30								
Tues.	8226	14	6/18	2 8		11/6½	30	30	7	50	103	3 / 3	45 / 45		10	4			5								
Wed.		5	3/32	11/40			"		8	8		6	28			1	32						8				
Thur.	92019	25	[illegible]/22	8/55	P.R.		52	20½	7	33	103	7	33		27												
Fri.	92208	16	12/34	7/35	P.R.		30	20½	7	1	88	7	1		59												
Sat.	5343 8712	SPL 1X88	9.24	5/30			"	30	8	6	103 REST DAY											4	36	3	30		
TOTAL								2-15	43	27		3 / 25	45 / 6	4	47	9	32		35			4	44	3	30		
Addition for Night Overtime and Sunday rate																2	23		12			2	22	2	37		

Hrs. 46 Mins. 20 Hrs. 13 Mins. 13

TOTAL Hours 61 Mins. 48

Pay No.	Signature	Rate	Computed Hours	Exps.
109	R.K. Graham	274/- 288/- 304/-	61¾	14/11 F.C. 7/6
	Grade P/Fireman	S.A.A.		

44 hour week adjustment
— hrs.
+ hrs.

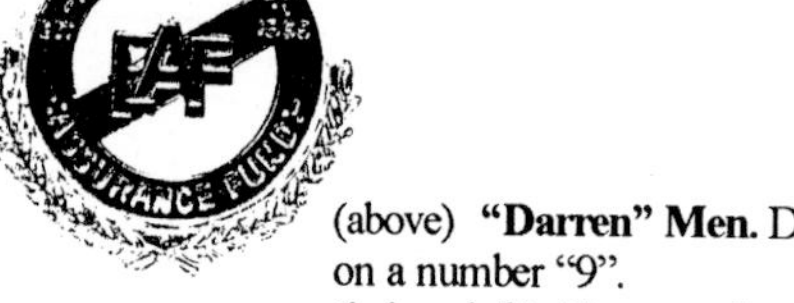

(above) **"Darren" Men.** Dave Hosker on a number "9".
(below left) Cleaners Gary Richards and Ken Smith.
(below right) Passed man Ben Nightingale and former Rose Grove fireman Mick Kelly on the Heysham - Hollins tank train. *Ron Graham / Mick Kelly.*

Lower Darwen M.P.D. (top) A hectic scene up at the "Delph", as engines shuffle about Lower Darwen shed in a view taken in the early 1950s. No.**42154** seen left, came brand new to "Darren" also seen are Nos.**44460** (of course) **90135** and **52299** and many more. (below) No.**76081**, one of the batch 76080 to 76084 which came new to the shed in the late 1950s. They were often borrowed to work excursions to the seaside. (left) Office staff line-up, (left to right) Arthur Sanders (shedmaster), Bill Archer (chief clerk), two unknown men and on the end George Higgett (R.S.F., later acting shedmaster). Behind them is bank engine No.**76083**. *John E Porter Bert Holland Frank Watson.*

Up at "The Delph"

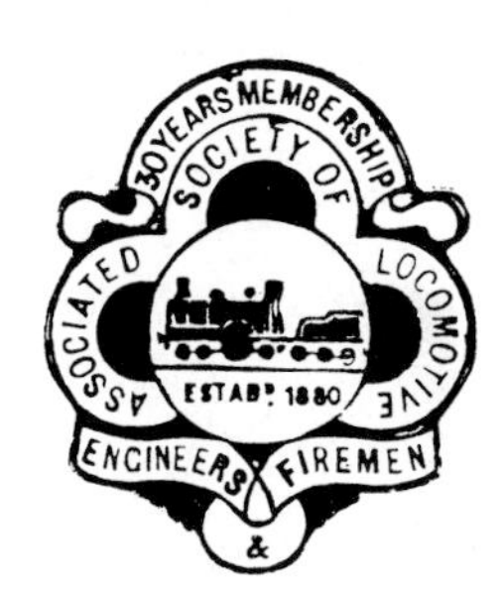

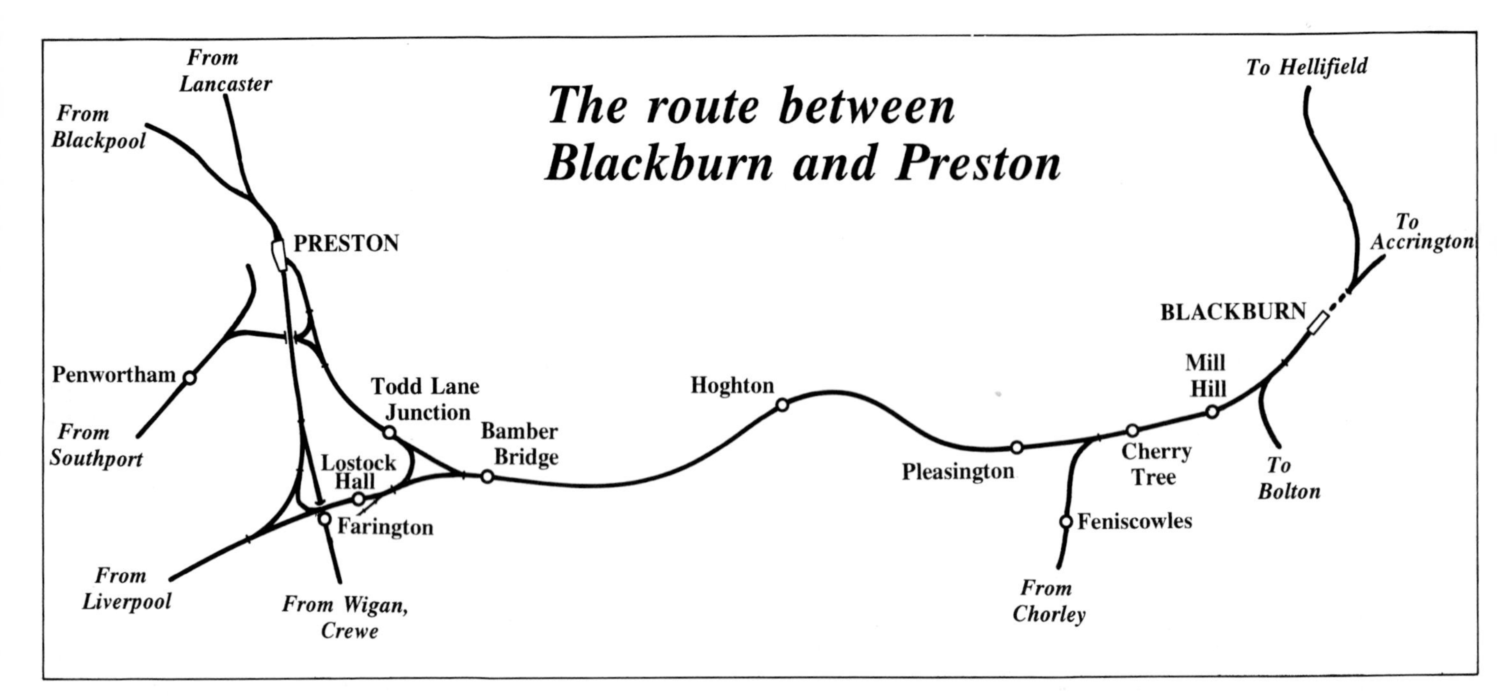

Blackburn to Bamber Bridge.

With the falling gradient at Blackburn station, only a little tugging by the loco. would be needed as the departure wave came. Soon we'd be trundling away down over Darwen Street bridge past the Bridge Sidings where Bert would shout across to us excitedly "there's a Crab over here, 42722" and sure enough one of Lower Darwen's "roughriders" would be simmering by the shunters cabin, it's crew down by the front end, where they would be sitting on the rail top soaking up the summer sun and eating their "butties" clearly enjoying a break from the heat of the engine's footplate. Further down the yard as we passed under the long iron bridge which spanned all the lines near to Bolton Junction signalbox, (Islington Bridge Road), one of "Darren's" Standard 4's No.76082 would be seen tapping wagons down the yard and "runners", the name given to those shunters who ran after the rolling wagons and pinned down the brakes, would be dashing along side the wagons riding them into the sidings. Of all jobs on the railway, their's must surely have been the most dangerous to be in. Of the Standard 4's, all of Lower Darwen's engines Nos.76080-84 would have at one time or another have been seen shunting here at Bolton Junction or as top points pilot further up round the bend on the Manchester line. At Bolton Junction, the line to Darwen, Bolton and ultimately Manchester, quickly curved away climbing up to the left. We would gather speed on the down grade towards Mill Hill and the sidings seen to our right would lead tightly away to the King Street coal yard, a very busy coal depot at this time. Just beyond where the lines headed for King Street, was Taylor Street High and Low Level goods yards together with a large warehouse. Yet more engines would be added to the pages of dad's notepad before we reached Mill Hill station. All around the railway at this point and far away towards the distant hills surrounding the town, rows of red brick terraced houses with narrow backstreets full of coal houses and outside "privvies" sat side by side, we were clearly in Coronation Street land! Every street corner seemed to sport an Off License or a chippy and you could sense it wasn't quite the local holidays yet, as lines of washing draped across the narrow streets blowing about in the warm summer air and we could see by the kids in the school yard close to Mill Hill that their summer term hadn't quite ended. On the run down to Mill Hill station, a goods line ran all the way on the Down side and for part of the way a blue brick retaining wall, complete with heavy iron rails like those on the Rose Grove humps, would act as a boundary marker for the railway. The line took a sweeping curve to the right on the run into Mill Hill station and here, towering over the station, was the large Waterfall Mill complex, which was situated to the right of the station's island platform. The mill looked striking in day time but more so at night, when it resembled a Christmas tree with its many neon lights advertising the firms activities as well as having all the many work floors illuminated, this dazzling array of lights could be seen some considerable distance away. Sometimes if we had called at Blackburn then another stop would ensue at Mill Hill. The platform was quite long containing some very rundown blackened red brick buildings over which was positioned a fair sized awning. The platform surface in places seemed to be made of blue bricks, the ones with a sort of tread pattern cast into them. The exit into Mill Hill was via a stairway which lead up to the main roadbridge above, this being at the Preston end of the station. If we did call at Mill Hill station, our driver accepted that the front coaches would be full by now and he would draw the first two or so coaches off the platform, (by arrangement with the guard), in order to be able the put the rear of the train on the platform. Due to the curve to the right at Mill Hill, the driver would have drawn his cab well clear of the station overbridge in order that his mate would be able to see the guard when he gave the tip from over on the Down side platform, rather than the platform where the train was standing. Mill Hill was only a short distance from another Blackburn suburb Cherry Tree and once away from Mill Hill the normal practice would be to get the train rolling and build up speed for the climb to Hoghton. A metal latticed footbridge lay half way between Mill Hill and Cherry Tree, it was a popular spot with kids, many of whom seemed to delight in throwing objects at the passing trains and so we always looked out at this point with some caution. The lineside around the footbridge tended to be littered with objects thrown off the bridge, these included kiddies bicycle frames,

continued on page 120

Mill Hill Station 11.8.64. No.**44686** enters Mill Hill with the 11.16am Saturdays only Colne to Southport train which ran via the West Lancs. route through Hesketh Bank etc. By arrangement with the guard the driver on long excursion trains would often run the odd coach off the platform end down by the bridge in the distance. *Bert Holland.*

Mill Hill was a station of contrasting styles. It did not follow the pattern of other stations between Blackburn and Preston, being a late arrival on the scene (1887). The policy of the L&Y at the time dictated that an island platform would suffice with a large "umbrella" type roof/awning covering the relevant areas. The end elevation (left-lower) shows the substantial framework of this type of roofing; the platform buildings contained waiting rooms, porters facilities, etc. At road level (below) there was a departure from the usual stylish red bricked entrance. In its place was this single storey flat roofed structure, somewhat austere but obviously functional. The year is 1953. *G. Biddle.*

Twixt Mill Hill and Cherry Tree stations. In brilliant sunshine No.**42297** ambles along to Mill Hill from Cherry Tree station, which can be seen beneath the overbridge in the distance. The closed Cherry Tree goods yard is to the right at this point. *Bert Holland*

old buckets, lumps of timber and building materials. Cherry Tree goods yard was situated over to the right and could be seen shortly after passing the footbridge, As you approached the station at Cherry Tree the yard was lost from view behind a large banking and only a brief glimpse of the goods warehouse was possible as we passed through the platform, only the blue slate roof of the goods shed could be seen. The goods yard closed from 1st April 1961 but the goods shed remains tucked away down the back to this day. Cherry Tree station platforms were split by an overbridge carrying a side road off the A 674 and the portions of the platforms on the Mill Hill side were rarely used and would be grassed over. Beyond the bridge however, an ornate wooden awning protected the passengers from the elements. The top part of it was painted in cream and the lower half in red. Over on the Down side a solid little stone built building acted as the main waiting area and booking hall, behind which was another goods shed built in stone, possibly from an earlier period in the railways history and from this a cobbled yard led up to the road bridge spanning the station. Picking up speed now and with the engine whistle shrieking as we flashed through Cherry Tree, it was nice for a change not to be stopping and starting. The iron bridge set at an angle to the railway and carrying the main A 674 passed above us as we clattered across Cherry Tree Junction. The line branching away here to the left climbed up the bank to Feniscowles, Brinscall and over to Chorley. Yet another rather ornate type of footbridge crossed all the lines at this point, more kids would be seen looking down at us as we sped past, but this time "the natives were friendly". There's even a chap taking our picture, I hope he's got a fast shutter speed! Still gaining speed we continued along the embankment which carried the railway in a straight line towards the delightful little station at Pleasington, its little flower beds were always neatly tended in those days. The loco.'s whistle shrieked out a warning as we leaned to the wide sweeping curve on the approach to Pleasington Golf Course. The links lay on both sides of the railway here and the whistling was to warn golfers who may be crossing the line. The whistle was also timed just right on some occasions, I say timed right, because some drivers would keep an eagle eye out for a golfer just teeing off and timing the whistle just right could sometimes throw the poor golfer off his stride and he'd send a lump of earth skywards instead of the ball! The golf course looked a picture in the summer sun. The many shades of green stood out so well. On we forged, our engine now tugging wildly at the coaches as the driver "dropped the gear" for the run up the bank to Hoghton. The roar at the chimney top increased and dark clouds from freshly fired coal headed skywards. On over the high arched viaduct at the bottom end of the bank we rattled, below us the river ran deep in the rocky gorge. Up the banking side we'd charge, the bark of the engine fading slightly as the driver became happier with the engines climbing performance. We settled down briefly to a steady pace of climb and soon we were passing the site of Tower Crossing where a signal box crossing and private sidings once stood. The blast at the chimney top sharpened as the driver

continued on page 124

Cherry Tree was one of the earliest stations in the area but did not initially come into use with the opening of the Blackburn & Preston Railway in 1846. The building shown here (9th March 1954) reflects contemporary methods of construction for the period although for many years, a canopy extended along the front of the building to the platform edge, with fitted barge boards decorating the gable ends. In the lower picture (13th September 1966), an unidentified Britannia heading east with a freight working, is framed by the arch of the overbridge. Note the profiled extension of the platform canopy, highlighting the restricted width of the platforms. *G. Biddle & P.E. Baughan.*

Cherry Tree Junction

Cherry Tree Junction. 1950s. Looking towards Cherry Tree station and Blackburn from the Chorley line at Cherry Tree Junction, Class 2 passenger loco. No.**40681** of Bolton shed drops down to the junction with a local working from Chorley which will probably be heading for Colne via the Great Harwood / Padiham Loop. *John E. Porter.*

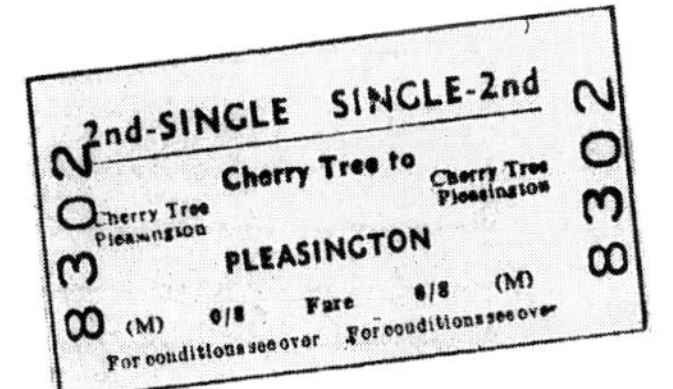

In the Woods. Surrounded by woodland and greenery Holbeck 5X, *Gwalior* bowls along in fine style just beyond Cherry Tree Junction, with 1X12 a Bradford - Blackpool working on 25.5.63. *Peter Fitton.*

Along the banking to Pleasington

(above). **S.O. Colne - Southport. 25.5.63.** Cantering along like a thoroughbred, my favourite engine, No.**75019** heads towards Pleasington with 2F79 the 11.16am from Colne, which passed Pleasington about 12.20pm each Saturday. *Peter Fitton.*

(below). **On the Chorley Line.** Riding along close to Pleasington we had this view of the line to Feniscowles and Chorley, here on 25.5.63 W.D. No. **90622** drops down to Cherry Tree Junction with empty wagons. *S.Taylor / Peter Fitton.*

Seahorse **at Pleasington. 25.5.63.** Blackpool's 5X, *Seahorse*, No.**45705** looks almost ex-works here at Pleasington in these two views of the 1.45pm S.O. Accrington to Blackpool Central. No.45705 seems to have worked this job a few times in May 1963 as two weeks earlier on the 11th we saw her parked on Rose Grove shed, ready to run light engine to Accrington. *Peter Fitton.*

Home Pass. No.**75046**, a former Accrington loco, now working from Bank Hall shed, stands in the Down platform at Pleasington with a return working from Southport to Colne. A year or two earlier, Colne passenger guard Bill Seed often worked a similar job to this using No.75046 and the other Accrington B.R. Standard Class 4's Nos.75045 - 49, where he would work to Preston then travel home as passenger to Colne at the end of his diagrammed work. *John E. Porter.*

continued from page 120

"gave it the last little bit" over the top. Once through the high arched bridge at Low Barn we topped the bank and our train began gaining momentum, again we were treated to the surging and tugging of the loco. just in front of us, like a puppy on a lead, it was eager to be away. The dark clouds of smoke from the engine had by now given way to billowing white clouds which drifted lazily across the fields to our right before evaporating in the warm summer air. It was over to the right as we rolled steadily towards Hoghton station that we were briefly treated to a wonderful view of the Ribble valley with its lush green fields and rolling hills that stretched for miles and miles into the far distance. Sadly, dad rarely saw this view, for mum and he would be busy as a rule at this point in the journey getting the flasks out and handing the egg sandwiches round. He only briefly stopped doing this to look out of the left side of the compartment. It was here at the top of the bank that a farmer had a number of long hen huts which stretched down near the line and literally hundreds of free range hens wandered about in the fields bordering the railway and so for a few moments dad was lost in the world of White Leghorns and Wine Dots. Speed increased further as we hit the crossover at Hoghton by the level crossing. The coach began to rock wildly causing dad to spill the tea he was pouring from the flask, "Blooming heck" he'd say, (or words of a stronger nature !) as the hot tea splashed on his shiny black shoes. Over on the other seat mum would chuckle at the happening as she cupped a flask lid full of steaming coffee in her hands. The run down to Bamber Bridge together with the section from Preston to Kirkham and Preston to Lancaster would normally be the fastest of our seaside trips. Hoghton's deserted station platform was passed in fine style, with barely a chance to view the station buildings which would fall quickly into decay with the closure of the station in September 1960. The compartment rocked from side to side as we headed down the hill flat out. The iron railings bordering the grounds of Brindle Lodge flashed by us, just a blur at speed. The dash down from Hoghton was short lived and by the time we past Hospital Crossing the rumble of the brake cylinders beneath the coach and the harsh grab of the brakes told us that the driver was getting hold of the train in readiness for the adverse signals that we would almost certainly encounter at Bamber Bridge. The line was almost straight from Hospital Crossing down to Bamber Bridge and as we looked forward in that direction the view of the wheels and motion of the loco. grew sharper as the speed fell. Ahead of us the Bamber Bridge home signals were firmly at danger and over in the distance the large Orr Mill stood high above the houses on the skyline. This huge textile mill with its many work floors was built very much in the style of those you would expect to see in the Oldham and Rochdale areas. It was constructed in red brick and had fancy towers on the corners, clearly it was Bamber Bridge's biggest land mark and could be seen for miles around from whichever direction you tended to approach. By the time we had reached the built up area of Bamber Bridge, speed was down to walking pace and in the late 1950s work was already in progress on the new M 6 motorway between Preston and Lancaster, and an ultra modern brick and concrete flyover would soon span the line at this point. The station was of course a junction and as such excursion traffic tended to queue for the routes ahead leading to the seaside, particularly it seemed if you were going in the Southport direction. We would always in that case stand for some time at the inner home signal near to the terraced row of houses of Cambridge Road. Through the streets there beyond the gable ends of the houses, we could see the imposing structure of Orr Mill. We would have to wait our turn to pass over Bamber Bridge level crossing which controlled movements on the busy main A 6 trunk road. The signal box

continued on page 128

Climbing "Hoghton Bank"

Firms Outing. Coming steadily up the bank at Hoghton is C895, a Blackpool bound works outing from Messrs. C.& W . Walmsley's Ltd., Three Brooks Mill at Oswaldtwistle. The date of this trip was Sunday 8th September 1957.
John E Porter.

Long Barn. Coming up through the high arched bridge at Long Barn near to the top of the bank at Hoghton a "Crab" is seen doing what they did best, steaming well and pulling hard. It was working the Saturdays only 7.15am Radford to Blackpool North train No.M19. This train which was booked to pass Hoghton summit at about 12.10pm, had come over Copy Pit and was routed round the Padiham loop.
John E Porter.

(above) **Hoghton Station.** A pair of "Accrington" sets, (DMU's) cruise through Hoghton level crossing on a Blackpool - Skipton working. (below) No.**44483** rattles a mixed bag of freight wagons through the tidy platforms at Hoghton on its run down the bank to Bamber Bridge. *Peter Fitton. / John E Porter.*

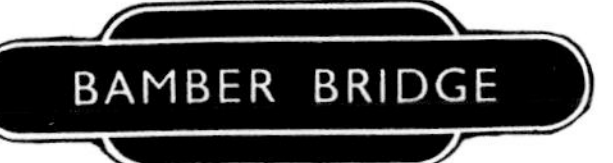

Bamber Bridge. The Up side platform buildings are seen here, looking back towards the level crossing over the busy A6 road. The subway, booking office etc. are all visible in this view. Road traffic grew enormously at Bamber Bridge and at the height of summer, what with all the extra trains, nobody envied the Bamber Bridge signalmans job. *G. H. Platt*

Down Side Buildings. Quite a solid stone structure formed the waiting rooms on the Down side at Bamber Bridge. In the back ground were the houses whose backyard walls reached right up to the platform surface. Near the level crossing on this Down side was a "chippy" and of course the "Lancs. and Yorks." public house, most handy for the station! *G. H. Platt.*

Relief of Enginemen and Guards working passenger and empty coaching stock trains not booked to call at Preston station, also provision of Conductors:—

Men booking on at Preston to act as Conductors or afford relief to up and down trains via Preston (E.L.) to be instructed to report to the Yard Foreman at Preston (E.L.), who will keep in touch with the E.L. Goods Yard Signalman and advise the men of the approach of the train they have to work. Men who travel to Preston to act as Conductors or afford relief to report direct to the Yard Foreman at Preston E.L. Goods Yard. The Signalman at Ribble Sidings and Preston E.L. Goods Yard boxes to advise the Signalman at Preston No. 5 signal box when up trains require Conductors or relief at Ribble Sidings and Preston (E.L.) respectively.

here was quite unique, being a tall slim structure with a flat roof. This most unusual of signalboxes was positioned on the Hoghton side of the level crossing, sitting closely up to the wall of a factory which stood next to the railway near to Cambridge Road. The elevated position of the signal box afforded excellent views of both the road and the railway. By the crossing stood the Lancs and Yorks. pub and also a popular little chip shop for which there always seemed an endless queue. The station platforms came right up to the edge of the crossing and with so much road and rail traffic passing this point, it was no wonder that the windows and paintwork on the subway were a grimy shade of brown under which lay a faded layer of red and cream paint. The platforms were flagged and the main station buildings over on the Up side were positioned close by the subway entrance. These included a booking office, waiting area and toilets all of dressed stone which due to the industrial surroundings had turned black over the years. The Down-side buildings were again of stone, but of much simpler design. Behind the Down-side platform sat the back yards of a row of red bricked terraces. The back yard walls of these houses were actually up to the platform itself. The goods yard over on the Up side of the line close to Bamber Bridge Junction was quite large in size and, as always, coal traffic played a major part of the yards activities. At Bamber Bridge Junction, the main route to the left took services to Liverpool and Southport (the latter branched off at Burscough) and trains also ran via Lostock Hall and Farington Junction to gain the West Coast main line to Wigan and Crewe. Those trains heading into Preston would pass through Lostock Hall station and continue via Farington Curve Junction, those for Liverpool would head out towards Moss Lane Junction and Midge Hall. Trains going into Preston would arrive there via the North Union or N. U. side. On our excursion trips, we rarely went that way and we would, as a rule, bear right at Bamber Bridge Junction and drop down past the exchange sidings at Brown Edge Crossing, run along to Todd Lane Junction and Whitehouse South Junction, from where we could turn left and head out to Hesketh Bank and Southport or continue down into Preston en-route to the coast via the East Lancs. side (Butler Street).

Our journey through East Lancashire by excursion train is now complete. We hope you have enjoyed the journey so far and look forward to your company in the next volume, when we will head out of Preston for the seaside.

STUART TAYLOR

September 7th 1962. Running out of Steam. Blackpool North (24E) based "Jubilee" No.**45681** *Aboukir* pauses en route with the last steam worked 4/30pm Colne to Blackpool Central (SX). On the footplate, Driver Eddie Smith and Fireman Derek Shackleton of Rose Grove. Join them in part two as we head for the coast. *Peter Fitton*